LISTEN
TO THE
UNIVERSE

A BEGINNER'S
GUIDE TO

SYNCHRONICITY

To all logical, rational, Cartesian people.
To the exclusively logical, rational and
Cartesian young lady that I once was.

LISTEN
TO THE
UNIVERSE

ANNE-SOPHIE CASPER

A BEGINNER'S
GUIDE TO

SYNCHRONICITY

DAVID & CHARLES

www.davidandcharles.com

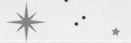

CONTENTS

INTRODUCTION 6

DISCOVERING
SYNCHRONICITY 11

WHAT IS SYNCHRONICITY? 12

Definition 12
Benevolent guides 13
7 examples of synchronicity 14
Chance, coincidence, miracle,
luck or magic? 16

ORIGINS AND MANIFESTATIONS 20

Paul Kammerer's law of seriality 20
Carl Jung, the father of
synchronicity 21
A tiny beetle makes great history 23
Joseph Campbell's praying mantis 24
Anthony Hopkins's book 24

UNDERSTANDING
SYNCHRONICITY 27

SYNCHRONICITY AND YOU 28

Test your relationship with
synchronicities 28
Tips to prepare for change 34

LIMITING BELIEFS AND
FALSE IDEAS ABOUT
SYNCHRONICITY 38

A DAY LIVING IN
SYNCHRONICITY 43

07:00, THE MORNING:
APPRECIATING SYNCHRONICITY 44

What is being anchored? 44
Finding your anchor point 45
We are all connected 46
The feather experiment 49
Your world map, your frame
of reference 50
Transforming your limiting beliefs 53

**12:00, LUNCHTIME: OBSERVING
SYNCHRONICITY**   56

Conducting the investigation   56
Developing your 5 senses   56
5 senses in 5 exercises   57
Test yourself!   58
Opening up your intuitive channel   63
Increasing your vibratory rate   63
Developing and training
the 6th sense   67

**17:00, TEATIME: DEEPENING
SYNCHRONICITY**   68

Playing with synchronicity   68
Discovering the different forms
of synchronicity   69
Using your intuition and...
no cheating!   86

**20:00, THE EVENING:
INTERPRETING SYNCHRONICITY**   92

The art of divination in the
service of your life   92
Discovering the I Ching, oracles
and bibliomancy   93
Your brilliant mental flexibility:
ASC and the trance state   100
Live deeply in the moment   103
The power of expressing gratitude   104
100% gratitude   105

**23:00, THE NIGHT: ATTRACTING
SYNCHRONICITY TO YOU**   106

Rendering the unconscious
conscious   106
The film of your day   108
The power of intention   108
Law of attraction: becoming
a magnet for synchronicities   110
Developing your positive thoughts
through premonitory dreams   112

FURTHER INFORMATION   **115**

CONCLUSION   116
ACKNOWLEDGEMENTS   119
BIBLIOGRAPHY   120
JOURNAL   122

INTRODUCTION

*All you have to do is to pay attention; lessons always arrive
when you are ready, and if you can read the signs, you will learn
everything you need to know in order to take the next step.*

PAULO COELHO

One particular significant event, which took place almost ten years ago, led me to consciously experience what Paulo Coelho is talking about. It was just after my very first coaching session as a coachee (I have been a personal and professional life coach, with a qualification from the Haute École de Coaching in Paris since 2016) that I discovered synchronicity. This discovery was a pivotal moment in my life, but it was not until a few years later that I became aware of its profound power. And I still have plenty more to learn! It is my belief that you need more than a single lifetime to penetrate all its mysteries.

In order to be as specific as possible, I think it is important for me to recount my experience to you. As the summer of 2012 drew to a close, after a particularly dark time in my life, I found myself in complete turmoil. After experiencing an acute professional disappointment and toxic relationships that drained me of all my energy, I was starting to have gloomy thoughts. As I walked with a friend along the bank of the River Seine in Paris, I described how I felt like the pebble that I had just thrown into the water: 'I am sinking because of all the idiots blocking my way forward.' I was not mincing my words,

because at the time I felt like a guerrilla fighter – faithless and lawless. My friend then told me about a meeting she had had with a life coach a few months earlier. She gave me her card. I took it with little conviction. I happened to notice that she had the same name as one of my aunts, Sylvie, also a life coach, and remarked to myself on the coincidence. This was just the start of several surprising coincidences. A few days later, I dropped my handbag as I went through the internal courtyard of my building and the caretaker shouted after me that I had left a business card behind on the floor. It was the life coach's card. The next day, I heard that my agent at the Entertainment Professionals Employment Agency, which supplied me with work, had just changed, and that the new one was called Sylvie. The chain of events was immediately cast in a new and lucky light: without thinking twice, I made an appointment for my first coaching session with the coach called Sylvie.

The following week, Sylvie greeted me with a welcoming smile. I will not detail precisely what went on in our first long meeting, but something real and beyond my control took me from 'I am paying you to sort out the problem of all these idiots around me', to 'OK, I want to trust you and give it a go, but if it doesn't work, you won't see me again'. I had (finally!) decided to stop hitting out and lay down my weapons. I didn't want to fight any more, I was done. At the time, I thought I was in control of everything, or nearly everything. So I wanted to give life a chance. Of course, it was only years later that I realised it was life that was offering me this wonderful opportunity to transform myself.

I left the session to head for a bookshop to buy the book Sylvie had recommended, *The Four Agreements* by Don Miguel Ruiz. Without really being aware of it, that was the day I opened the door to signs, to joy and to life's positive surprises. I was never to close it again. That week, in autumn 2012, remains ingrained in my memory.

Using brainpower alone, I then prepared a long list for my coach of the positive things that had happened to me in the course of that week, quite beyond my control! I couldn't believe it! My mind was in turmoil, 'How is this possible? Does this really happen to everyone? Was I just lucky? Is this a magic trick or mere chance?' Now it makes me laugh to look back at my too numerous questions. I even asked my coach if she had paid these people to be kind, welcoming and pleasant to me! As I mentioned, I really was very cerebral and Cartesian. To believe it, I needed to have real evidence. The Universe had listened to me and responded to my requests.

Putting out positive vibes and giving life the opportunity to surprise me had immediately allowed me to reap some beautiful human experiences. These ranged from a simple door being held open by a stranger and the paying of compliments (which is quite rare in Paris), to a call for work and the discovery of a ten-euro note stuck to the sole of my shoe! Week by week, I discovered with wonder the simplicity, accessibility, potency and power of synchronicity.

One does not become enlightened by imagining figures of light, but by making the darkness conscious. The latter procedure, however, is disagreeable and therefore not popular.
CARL GUSTAV JUNG

Sharing my experience through this book (and indeed all the books that I have written) is very important to me. My heartfelt aim is to bring you awareness to enable you to open your heart, body, mind and soul by humbly laying before you my discoveries, experiences and knowledge. I do not claim to be privy to the one, sole truth about synchronicity, because I, too, am a human being in the process of evolution. Like each one of us, I succeed, I fail and I learn every day. However, I share with you the truth that is mine today with authenticity, sincerity and kindness.

In the first two sections of this book, you'll discover synchronicity and understand it a little more, and in the third section I'll invite you to spend a day getting your head around the concept: observing, deepening, interpreting and attracting synchronicity to you. If you are reading this, it is more than likely that you wish (consciously or otherwise) to make time for yourself, so here's the perfect opportunity to do just that. For 24 hours, take your time, respecting your inner dynamic equilibrium and personal rhythm. Don't forget, there is no such thing as chance. I wish you illumination in your reading.

DISCOVERING SYNCHRONICITY

The personal growth market has been booming for several years now. As a consequence, the notion of synchronicity has made a triumphant return to bookshop shelves catering to esotericism and personal development. However, like any ancient concept, as it travels down the years, its initial meaning becomes distorted and modified.

In this first section, I will seek to define synchronicity for you. So what is it exactly? Is there a difference between the notions of chance, coincidence, miracle, luck and magic? These are some of the questions that the first section of this book will answer.

WHAT IS SYNCHRONICITY?

With the aim of total transparency, the first thing I want to do is lift the veil on the definition of synchronicity. It would be very presumptuous of me to state that we have a perfect knowledge of what it is. A mysterious power? A magical phenomenon? In my opinion, no author or expert can claim to know the truth about the concept of synchronicity. This is likewise the case with regard to its origins and history. In reality, such knowledge is not yet sufficiently clear and precise to be accepted by everyone.

DEFINITION

The dictionary definition of synchronicity is the 'simultaneous occurrence of two or more events that are not causally related, but whose association makes sense to the person who perceives them'. The principle of synchronicity is illustrated in the perfect alignment of our thoughts, our words and the reality we are having in the moment. The experience of synchronicity lies in the meaning ascribed to this acausal, uncontrollable, impalpable and unmanageable manifestation by a (sane and balanced) human being.

For example, shortly before the idea for this book was born, I noticed in Quebec, where I live, many signs that prompted me to write to one of my French editors, with whom I had not been in contact for a long time. On the other side of the Atlantic, from her office in Paris, she told me that she had just been talking about me and that she had been thinking of writing to me for several days to suggest this book. Some people will see this as a happy coincidence, the probability of which is very low. Others will assign a deeper meaning to this anecdote, as it perfectly illustrates the power of synchronicity. Personally I saw it as a knowing wink from the Universe to encourage me to write on this subject.

While the ranks are swelling of those of us who believe in synchronicity and these manifestations of events (repetitive or otherwise) with no apparent cause, my goal here is not to convince you. My aim is to share my point of view with you, with total sincerity. In my opinion, synchronicity exists to give us an answer to a question; to provide confirmation, encouragement, a divine message; but

Those who learn nothing from the unpleasant facts of life force the cosmic consciousness to reproduce them as many times as necessary to learn what the drama of what happened teaches. What you deny submits you; what you accept transforms you.
CARL GUSTAV JUNG

also to pass on some teaching or remind us not to deviate from our life's path. It is precious help from which we can all benefit, without distinction.

The concept of synchronicities is steeped in psychology, quantum physics, mysticism and spirituality. This is why believers often see them as signs from God, or from guardian angels, of guiding lights, or from certain deities. Regardless of our spiritual obedience and practice, these signs of life confirm our interconnectedness and the intuitive capacity which we all effortlessly possess.

As we are all linked and connected to each other, we alternate between being messengers and receivers, without even consciously seeking to do so.

BENEVOLENT GUIDES

Synchronicities accompany us along our path in life, without judgement, advice or orders to follow, like mountain guides or tour guides, or life, personal or professional coaches. It is up to each individual

whether they want them by their side and whether they choose to use their support in case of difficulty to help get back on track. Synchronicities are, in my opinion, wonderful tools for (re)alignment, (re)motivation, and help with confidence-building (in oneself, in others and in life). The symbolic resonances of synchronicities connect us with that which we do not yet perceive and which will enter our consciousness in the near or more distant future.

Etymologically, the term 'synchronicity' comes from the Greek 'syn' (meaning 'with') and 'chronos' (meaning 'time'). I like to say that synchronicity is a waltz between time and the spirit. We are free to remain a spectator of this dance or to participate in it and, step by step, follow the music of life.

One of the difficulties I have found in experiencing this particular phenomenon lies in capturing all the synchronicities presented to me, without missing any. It is the same for everybody. These days we are literally bombarded with messages and information from morning to night. This makes it difficult for our brain to identify, filter, analyse, sort and store them. In addition, our minds are influenced by several significant factors (our natural intellectual capacity, our beliefs, our openness, our environment and our emotions), which greatly affect how vigilant we are able to be.

7 EXAMPLES OF SYNCHRONICITY

I am sure you are already wondering about your own experiences with this mysterious phenomenon of synchronicity.In order to focus your thoughts, I have set out a list of seven examples of synchronicities in everyday life. In the third section of this book (A Day Living In Synchronicity, page 43),

I suggest that you explore them in more depth, experienced through the course of a whole day dedicated to synchronicity.

✸ **You think of a particular person who is dear to you and, bang, just like that...** you hear their first name (on the radio, on a television advert, in a film, or in someone else's conversation) or you read it (on a shop front, in an email, on the side of a bus). This event can happen repeatedly in a fairly short period of time. For example, you hear a song when you turn on your car radio, then you go into a shop and find the CD the song is on.

✸ **You have a serious problem to which you have not managed to find a solution.** In some surprising way, over which you have had no control, life offers you the solution by stimulating one or more of your five senses (sight, hearing, taste, smell, touch).

✸ **You remember a significant event or situation where you were not alone,** then you receive a phone call, a text message or an email from someone who was a participant in that moment in your life.

✸ **You are feeling down, a bit depressed,** you may even be thinking dark thoughts... Yet on that day, a particularly kind word (from a shop assistant, a neighbour or a delivery person, perhaps), or a defining encounter or something very special comes along to remind you that life is good.

✸ **You ask yourself an important question** (internally or out loud) and hear the answer when you turn on the radio, or when watching a television programme or reading the title of a book.

✸ **You wake up in the middle of the night in a panic** and/or have a nightmare that someone in your family is in serious trouble. You go back to sleep and find out the next day that this has really happened.

✸ **You need to make an important choice,** but you are torn between various options. A set of circumstances conspires naturally to guide you towards the right path. These circumstances may also confirm your initial feeling in order to push you in the best direction.

This last example reminds me of a decisive event in my career transition a few years ago. I had just obtained my certification as an image consultant. Even though I had joined the personal shopping department of a major store for a few hours a week, I had severe doubts about my professional future. I was wondering whether I should go back to full-time work in the media and just do image consultancy work in my free time. At that moment, I was woken (both literally and figuratively!) by a telephone call. It was Charlotte, a well-known image consultant whom I had met two years earlier when I worked in the television industry. I had had no news of her since. She told me that she had been closely following my career change on social media and had a proposal to make to me. She said that we were going to 'swap roles' and announced that she was about to become a television presenter! She would not have time for her luxury clientele and wanted to pass them on to someone she trusted – namely me. I was lost for words... I even tried to convince her not to take me on by telling her that I had not been in the profession long enough to take over from her! I came to my senses, however, and accepted her proposal. We worked together on an initial job, then I took on her client list alone. These first major contracts that fell into my lap were the start of an amazing adventure. They were particularly pivotal. Without them, I would perhaps never have embarked professionally down this road.

The power of synchronicities is unlimited and can multiply, just like a Russian doll. In fact, there is another interesting facet to this anecdote. When I met Charlotte in 2013, I was the project manager for the pilot of a particular television programme. The concept was simple: two professionals had the job of helping a young woman achieve a specific objective. Charlotte advised her on her look and Pascal gave the psychological input as her life coach. Did you know that as well as qualifying as an image consultant in 2014, I also achieved certification allowing me to become a personal and professional life coach in 2016? If you had said to me while we were filming that programme that three years later, I would be pursuing the professions of the two people involved in the making of that programme, I would not have believed you! But this is indeed what happened.

Since then, I have often felt like Hop o' My Thumb , a character in a fairytale by Charles Perrault, who, abandoned by his impoverished parents deep in the forest, leads himself and his brothers back home by following a trail of small white pebbles he has laid on his way to the woods. I 'just' pick up the pebbles that life puts in my path. If we open our eyes and ears, I profoundly believe that we can all be Hop o' My Thumb in our lives.

CHANCE, COINCIDENCE, MIRACLE, LUCK OR MAGIC?

What is the difference between these five concepts? Is synchronicity chance or magic? Can we say that it consists of coincidences or miracles, or that it is simply luck? To make things clearer, I would like you to do the exercise on the facing page.

I agree with certain schools of thought that define chance as something that is surprising and unpredictable. On the other hand, it does not shake up our lives in the same way that synchronicity does. One might think that coincidence – the literal explanation of which is 'co' meaning 'with' and 'incidence' meaning 'event' – is similar to synchronicity. However, there is a big difference between the two. Coincidences may surprise or amuse us, but their impact is not that great. When the power of synchronicity kicks in, it has major and significant effects. It can change the course of our existence. We are not talking here about a simple meeting with someone you bump into, but rather coming across someone who will have a particularly major impact on your life. Synchronicity is the lining up of coincidences that are meaningful

YOUR TURN TO PLAY

Match the five dictionary definitions (A–E) with the five descriptions (1–5). You'll find the answers at the base of the page.

USE YOUR INTUITION AND... NO CHEATING!

A. A set of powerful beliefs and practices based on the idea that there are hidden powers of nature. The aim is to reconcile them or conjure them up in order to bring good or bad luck. ○

○ **1.** CHANCE

B. A phenomenon interpreted as a divine intervention, the result of which is extraordinary and arouses admiration. ○

○ **2.** COINCIDENCE

C. A circumstance of an unforeseen or unpredictable nature, which may have a favourable or unfavourable effect on someone. ○

○ **3.** MIRACLE

D. A total stroke of fortune, a happy outcome to something or a favourable situation for someone. ○

○ **4.** LUCK

E. A completely fortuitous intersection of circumstances and events that occur at the same time. ○

○ **5.** MAGIC

Answers: A-5, B-3, C-1, D-4 and E-2

for the person who experiences them. Synchronic events are beautiful gifts from the Universe, experienced when they first appear as genuine small miracles, because they are not rational, intelligible or explicable. This is why this concept is so specific and so 'strange'.

According to Caroline de Surany, author of *La Chance, quel talent!* [translates to: *Luck, what talent!*], 'Luck is when everything that happens to you seems impossible or very improbable.' Luck – whether it is heads or tails, a stroke of good fortune, or a case of hard luck – even if it can be triggered or attracted, does not have the same depth as synchronicity. In terms of the extraordinary, miracles only occur very rarely. The people who are on the receiving end of them are then perceived as the chosen ones, insiders or out-of-the-ordinary beings. By contrast, synchronicities are universal. They are not particular to any specific age, colour, culture or social class. We can all, without distinction, benefit from their incredible potency. Divine power and action are totally exterior and there is no accountability on the part of the person who experiences a miracle. Despite prayers, requests or incantations seeking healing, the person who is the subject of the miracle has no control or material impact on what happens to them. By contrast, to activate the power of synchronicity, it is essential to be a co-actor. Without this, nothing will happen to us... seemingly.

Magic is the soul at work. As a result, some people will tell me that the power of synchronicity is in some way magic. However unlike magic, synchronicity is not associated with the sphere of illusion and the spectacular. Sometimes, synchronicity can be very simple and of a very limited duration.

A WINK FROM THE UNIVERSE

When life, the Universe (or any other representation that resonates with your personal frame of reference) gives us a little nod via the phenomenon of synchronicity, it is to confirm that we are the right person, connected to the right time and right place.

02

ORIGINS AND MANIFESTATIONS

It is to Carl Gustav Jung, Wolfgang Ernst Pauli and Paul Kammerer that we owe the principle of synchronicity as we know it today. From Jung's beetle to Joseph Campbell's praying mantis to Anthony Hopkins's book, the manifestations of this phenomenon make it ever more mysterious.

PAUL KAMMERER'S LAW OF SERIALITY

In his 1831 short story 'The Conscript', Honoré de Balzac wrote, 'These observations, collected with scientific curiosity by a few isolated individuals, will one day serve as documents on which to base the foundations of a new science which hitherto has lacked its man of genius.' This genius could be Paul Kammerer (1880–1926), an Austrian biologist and zoologist who at the turn of the 20th century was making lists of concordant events, highlighting similar numbers, dreams, names, or themes. He came up with a means of classifying this **'law of seriality'** by area and by number of points in common (2, 3, 4, 5 or even 6). Among the most incredible, Paul Kammerer describes that in 1915, two volunteer soldiers with pneumonia were admitted to the same military hospital on the same day: they were both 19 years old, both born in Silesia (Poland) and both named Franz Richter.

NEVER TWICE WITHOUT THRICE!

In 1919, Paul Kammerer published the results of his research, consisting of statistical analyses. The scientist concluded that there was an inexplicable force in the Universe that attracted and grouped things together by similarity and affinity. The law of seriality 'never twice without thrice' would therefore be real. After reading Kammerer's conclusions, Albert Einstein is said to have described them as 'interesting and by no means absurd'.

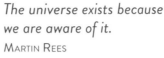

The universe exists because we are aware of it.
MARTIN REES

The story about the Franz Richters reminds me of my first day in year 11 at secondary school. I was new. When I went to collect my locker number and key, I was told that they could not give me a second key because I had already signed for one. Rather perturbed, I decided to go and take a look and found that a girl in the final year was using my locker. After a bit of awkwardness, we realised that we both had the same first and last names. Incredible, isn't it?

CARL JUNG, THE FATHER OF SYNCHRONICITY

Carl Gustav Jung, Swiss psychiatrist (1875–1961), was the founder of analytical psychology. He was one of the first disciples of Sigmund Freud who studied the mechanisms of the individual unconscious mind and came up with some major new concepts (individuation, psychological types, active imagination).

Dr. Jung conducted extensive studies on the phenomenon of synchronicity. It is notably as a result of these studies that the term **collective unconscious** was born. According to Dr. Carl Jung, synchronicity is an 'acausal [or non-causal] connecting principle.' Its particular nature is therefore not that it is part of a process of cause and effect, but of a system in which two events are linked only by the meaning we give them.

The information provided by the synchronicity is considered to be linked to the collective unconscious. It is not personal and individual. The collective unconscious brings together the unconscious minds of our communities, families, countries and the groups we belong to. These sets of individuals (and the sum of the individual information stored by each) make up the collective unconscious. Located in another dimension (outside of space-time), some experts define the collective unconscious as the 'memory of humanity', the 'memory of the soul' or the 'cosmic supraconsciousness of the Universe'. It is notably composed of archetypes common to all, which are centres of psychic energy. These may be symbols, images or formulae – a cross, a sun, a Star of David, a Flower of Life, a magic wand or a Tarot card.

When we open ourselves to the field of possibilities of synchronicity, we connect with each other in a dimension other than the one in which we consciously evolve.

Some people consider Carl Gustav Jung to be the co-creator of the **concept of synchronicity** alongside Wolfgang Ernst Pauli (1900–1958), a renowned Austrian physicist and mathematician (who was awarded the Nobel Prize in Physics 1945). Their long correspondence and their joint work, *Synchronicity: an Acausal Connecting Principle* (1952), map out the four fundamental laws of the *unus mundus* (the 'one world', a medieval alchemical concept in which there is no distinction between the psychic and physical spheres).

Using the psychophysical diagram below, they explain that synchronicity is the missing dimension required to achieve a complete understanding of the psyche and the physis (i.e., nature). This figure illustrates the perfect balance that allows harmony between the four fundamental laws of life.

✴ Causality represents the constant relationship of events by the production of effects.
✴ The space-time continuum comprises four dimensions (three dimensions for space and one for time).
✴ Indestructible energy is impalpable, immaterial, indissoluble and unfailing.
✴ Synchronicity is the phenomenon defined on page 12.

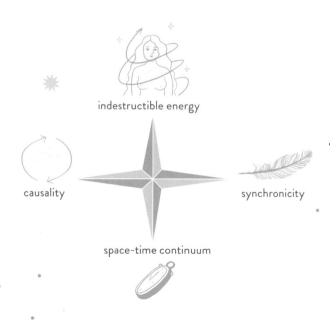

indestructible energy

causality

synchronicity

space-time continuum

The story goes that Dr. Jung made an in-depth study of the Chinese divinatory art of I Ching (in simplified Chinese 易经 and in traditional Chinese 易經), based on the book of the same name, also known as the *Book of Changes* or *The Classic of Changes*. As a result of his discoveries, he organised and made a real theory of his thoughts on synchronicities. Of the I Ching, he wrote that it is 'based not on the causality principle but on one which – hitherto unnamed because not familiar to us – I have tentatively called the synchronistic principle.'

Since the late 1940s, many therapists and practitioners of Jungian analytical psychology have been fascinated by the power of synchronicities. To learn more about their work, I recommend starting with the best-selling book by Quebecker psychologist Jeff Vézina, *Necessary Chances*.

A TINY BEETLE MAKES GREAT HISTORY

Taken from the biography of Carl Gustav Jung, the beetle anecdote is a perfect illustration of the power of synchronicity. During one psychoanalysis session, one of Dr. Jung's patients (a hyper-rational thinker) recounted her dream in which someone had given her the gift of a golden scarab. At that very moment, an insect flew into the glass behind Jung. He opened the window, caught it, and placed it on the table in front of him. And what sort of insect do you think it was? It was a small beetle, more precisely a golden scarab beetle. Merely a coincidence? A chance, well-timed occurrence? The patient became completely overwhelmed emotionally. This little creature, guided by the Universe and the collective unconscious, allowed her to envisage this experience in a different, more poetic and symbolic way. According to Jung, who made the link between this synchronicity and the inner transformation that had now been triggered in his patient, she seized the opportunity and immediately understood the profundity of this phenomenon in her life.

I wish you all moments like this. Dare to let yourself be overwhelmed by what you do not yet understand. Dare to trust your inner self. Dare to open yourself to new and as yet unknown notions. Dare to let yourself be swept along by things, events and relationships.

THE SYMBOLISM OF THE SCARAB

The scarab beetle is an important symbol, held sacred by the ancient Egyptians as it represented rebirth, fertility and protection. A scarab was placed on the heart of the deceased during embalming as a good luck charm to bring strength, courage and abundance. The animal served to guide the dead person to the afterlife.

JOSEPH CAMPBELL'S PRAYING MANTIS

Another interesting animal when it comes to the principle of synchronicity is the praying mantis. In another atypical situation, but very similar to the Dr. Jung scarab anecdote, Joseph Campbell (1904–1987), the American mythologist, anthropologist and writer, had an experience that he was to remember for a long time! Campbell was writing a book entitled *The Way of the Animal Powers*, and had just begun a chapter on the Kalahari Bushmen. The story goes that just as he was writing what an important place the praying mantis occupies in the mythology of this African tribe, he opened the window of his apartment in a New York tower block and saw a praying mantis, something he had never seen before! He later wrote, 'Its face looked like the face of a Bushman. It gave me the creeps!' Again, was it just a coincidence, given that he was writing these words on the 14th floor of a Manhattan high-rise?

THE SYMBOLISM OF THE PRAYING MANTIS

A symbol of mastery, patience, silence and equilibrium, the term 'mantis' comes from the ancient Greek word *mantis* meaning prophetess. The praying mantis has a potent power of quietude and immobility.

ANTHONY HOPKINS'S BOOK

In 1973, Anthony Hopkins landed a role in the film adaptation of *The Girl from Petrovka* (written by George Feifer in 1971). In order to prepare himself properly, the actor searched for the book in several London bookshops, without success. Just as he had decided to go home, before he went down to the underground, his eyes were drawn to a book lying on a bench. He went over, and which book do you think it was? *The Girl from Petrovka*, of course! Anthony Hopkins was flabbergasted. It seemed impossible, but it was true! Yet the power of synchronicity in this story does not end there. A few months later, on the set of the film in Vienna, the actor met the author in person. Hopkins began to tell Feifer his incredible anecdote and about his difficulty in getting hold of a copy of his book. The writer told him that he had only had one copy himself. But most unluckily, one day he had lent it to a friend who had had it stolen from his car. When Hopkins took out his copy (some passages of which were annotated), Feifer recognised it... as his own! The story came full circle.

Above and beyond the spectacular and impressive aspect of these famous anecdotes, I have chosen these three stories to share with you to demonstrate the power of the phenomenon of synchronicities. Of course, these examples are by no means the only ones – there are thousands of them! So keep your eyes and ears open!

IN SUMMARY

Synchronicity is distinct from chance, coincidence, miracle, luck and magic.

The principle of synchronicity is illustrated in the perfect alignment of our thoughts, our words and the reality we are experiencing at the same time. The experience of synchronicity lies in the meaning ascribed to this acausal, uncontrollable, impalpable and unmanageable manifestation.

Synchronicities are forged of psychology, quantum physics, mysticism and spirituality. This is why believers often see them as signs from the Divine, regardless of their spiritual persuasion and practices.

The concept of synchronicity connects us all via the collective unconscious (as illustrated by the anecdotes of Jung, Campbell and Hopkins). We are constantly alternating between the position of messenger and receiver without even the conscious desire to do so.

Carl Gustav Jung, Swiss psychiatrist (1875–1961), was the founder of analytical psychology and the father of synchronicity. He can be credited with having created this concept alongside Wolfgang Ernst Pauli (1900–1958), the Austrian physicist and mathematician (Nobel Prize in Physics 1945).

UNDERSTANDING SYNCHRONICITY

In the second part of this book, I want to help get you into the best possible place to assimilate and deepen the power of synchronicities. To do so, I am going to provide you with some specific tools which will help meet your needs, and attract every opportunity to experience synchronicities.

In addition, by unpicking any misconceptions about this phenomenon, we can shed light on any limiting beliefs that you may have or hurdles you may have to overcome in order to live a full day of synchronicity (see page 43).

01

SYNCHRONICITY AND YOU

Synchronicities are the jokers in nature's pack of cards for they refuse to play by the rules and offer a hint that, in our quest for certainty about the Universe, we may have ignored some vital clues.

FRANCIS DAVID PEAT

Is this really the right time to open yourself up to synchronicities? To confirm that the answer is 'Yes!', or to help you find the ideal moment, I invite you to take the following tests.

TEST YOUR RELATIONSHIP WITH SYNCHRONICITIES

Take a deep breath and read the following statements calmly. Being completely honest and transparent with yourself, tick the ones that apply to you. Complete each test, filling in how many statements you agree with in the boxes provided. Add the four totals and find out your result.

MY STATE OF MIND

○ I am an optimistic person who prefers to see the glass half full than half empty.

○ People think of me as caring, kind and interested.

○ The people around me think of me as enthusiastic, dynamic and up for a good time.

○ I find it easy to get things in perspective and can see the positive in every experience.

○ I like learning new methods and trying out new techniques to get to know myself better and to challenge myself in order to evolve.

○ I am sociable and at ease in company, but I can be an excellent observer.

○ I enjoy silence and feel at ease with it, whatever the situation.

○ I seek to learn from every obstacle or challenge that comes my way.

○ I like receiving presents, but most especially giving them. People think of me as generous.

○ I can let go very easily whenever I want to and feel mentally stable.

TOTAL 1

MY EQUILIBRIUM AND MY NEEDS

○ I like taking my time and not leaving things to the last minute.

○ I recognise, welcome and fulfil my desires when I feel the need.

○ Even though life is not always easy, I try to learn from every experience it brings me.

○ To stay balanced, I practise yoga, meditation, centering or relaxation.

○ I know how to define my needs and priorities in order to do justice to their true value.

○ In general, I follow things through: I follow my dreams and achieve my goals.

○ I like meeting new people and discovering new subjects and hobbies.

○ I pay close attention to ensuring a healthy balance between the most important areas of my life (personal, family, intimate, professional, social, etc.).

○ I take my share of responsibility and do not lay the blame on others: my choices are 100% my own.

○ Interaction with others seems essential to me: it is important for me to talk to others and share our thoughts.

TOTAL 2

MY EMOTIONS

◯ On the whole I try to acknowledge and listen to my emotions, even when they are intense.

◯ I know and practise anchoring so I am not thrown off balance by my emotions.

◯ I am generally calm and nothing can disturb my serenity.

◯ I feel psychologically stable because my mental health is good and well-balanced.

◯ I do not feel put out by negative people and/or events.

◯ I find it easy to let myself go with the flow and be guided by my emotions.

◯ I like tuning in to, feeling and expressing my emotions.

◯ I am sensitive and live intensely, but not hypersensitive to the extent of losing my footing.

◯ No event (past or present) disturbs me anymore.

◯ I know that my emotions are neither positive nor negative, but are calls for me to react quickly.

TOTAL 3

MY RELATIONSHIP WITH THE PARANORMAL

○ I believe in God, deities or a power greater than living beings.

○ I have always been fascinated by magic tricks, illusion shows and the effects of trances (hypnotic, shamanic, etc.).

○ I believe in near-death experiences.

○ People would describe me as having the same capacity for wonder as a child.

○ I think that our existence has a meaning and that there is a reason for everything.

○ I have in the past consulted a clairvoyant or medium to find out about my future or communicate with someone who has passed.

○ I am particularly sensitive to energies and vibrations (of humans, animals, nature, places or music).

○ When I listen to my feelings and my intuition, it brings only positive results.

○ I like new, original, surprising and unusual experiences.

○ I believe that everyone has extrasensory abilities (clairvoyance, clairsentience, precognition, etc.).

TOTAL 4

RESULTS

☀ If you have ticked 32 statements or more

In answer to the question, 'Is this really the right time to open yourself to synchronicities?', you can give a resounding 'Yes!' This is the ideal moment. You are more than ready! Be grateful and thank your intuition that led you to buy this book. Later in the book, I will give you all the tools you need to enjoy a full 24 hours of synchronicity (see page 43). All the same, I would suggest you integrate all the moments of this unique day one by one. Integration must be done step by step. To retain your excellent personal equilibrium, take a look at my recommendations on page 34, Tips to Prepare for Change.

☀ If you have ticked between 20 and 31 statements

You have a good, strong, solid base to experience synchronicities without being overwhelmed by their power. Congratulations! If your test totals are consistent, you have everything you need to optimise the favourable aspects of your life. I advise you to concentrate on your weaker areas. You will gain the confidence and peace of mind you need to tackle this day of 100% synchronicity from a firm footing!

☀ If you have ticked 19 statements or fewer

Above all else, don't be disappointed or sad. I would ask you, without judgement, to look deeply inside yourself. On a scale of 0 to 10, how do you feel at the moment? If you are still curious and happy, don't give up. Remember what brought you to this book. The Universe is there for a reason. So grasp the opportunity to follow this experience through to the end. Why is it important for you to discover the phenomenon of synchronicities? To achieve your goal, whatever that may be, take action by putting into practice the suggestions I have set out in the following pages. Take your time to assimilate them and go at your own pace. If this is your path, the perfect moment will come, be it in an hour, a day, or a year. Remember the words of Paul Éluard who said, 'There is no such thing as chance, only encounters.'

TIPS TO PREPARE FOR CHANGE

Wanting to change is all very well. But taking the action required to actually do so is even better! I have set out below my advice on cultivating a positive state of mind, finding your equilibrium and fulfilling your needs, but also on welcoming and managing your emotions to open yourself to the paranormal.

🐾 Cultivating an open state of mind

By their nature, humans are not drawn to things that lie outside of their personal frames of reference. Openness is, therefore, not a given for everyone. Children who are brought up in a formal household, discouraged by their parents from being open to certain ideas, or sharing their parents' unconscious fears, will in turn become blinkered adults. If you identify with this in any way, remember everything in life can change and be transformed if the desire is really there to do so. The secret is to reach where you want to be step by step and at your own pace.

The successful ascent of a high mountain, daunting though it may seem, requires one to be prepared and to take it step by step. Opening your mind is the same. Start by observing minor things in your day-to-day life. Like Sherlock Holmes, **be attentive and demonstrate curiosity** about the things around you. What colour outfit was your partner wearing this morning? What was the title of the book that the person sitting next to you on the bus was reading?

Take every opportunity that presents itself to learn and explore new things. If you are quick to pass judgement, replace your preconceived ideas and limiting convictions with open questions in order to find out more. Behind every behaviour, every utterance and every word, there hides a reason – and even if you do not share that reason, accept that it has the right to exist.

I am convinced that there is a positive glimmer inside even the most pessimistic of us, and I urge you to **develop your positivity**. As with the concept of yin and yang, there is always a little piece of white in the black and vice versa. Being positive does not mean being naive or in denial, of course. Quite the contrary in fact! Positivity is having the ability to see and understand that every experience or challenge is an opportunity to learn. From the moment we start to see what it has to offer, the reward system in our brain is triggered and we want more! By training the positivity muscle, we will strengthen a virtuous circle. The more we think positively, the more the possibility that we can live in a positive world. As Buddha said, 'We are what we think. All that we are arises with our thoughts. With our thoughts, we make the world.'

🐾 Meeting your needs and finding your equilibrium

As I explain in my book *Le Guide des Soins Énergétiques* [translates to: *A Guide to Energy Healing*], to maintain harmonious and healthy balance in your life, it is essential that your needs are met. If they are not met, they linger, dragging you down and preventing you from taking action. When they are fulfilled, they are incredible sources of joy and energy.

Unlike cravings, which are ephemeral desires, needs will remain as necessities and requirements if they are not met. For example, you might crave a bar of chocolate, but need to fill an emotional void. You should be able to forget your craving for something sweet without too much difficulty, but your need for affection cannot be glossed over. To help you establish and prioritise your needs, the American psychologist Abraham Maslow (1908-1970), created **the hierarchy of needs**, visualised as the pyramid below. This is an interesting tool for establishing your priorities and focusing on them effectively – your very own mountain to climb!

The other important concept in terms of finding your equilibrium is letting yourself **go with the flow**. This is very fashionable currently, but I sometimes read that some people equate it with a lax attitude, yet, as far as I am concerned, the complete opposite is the case. Going with the flow is anything but being passive and giving in. Indeed, it is leads us to live more consciously so we can be active in our choices to act more effectively.

If the words 'impossible' and 'inaccessible' keep popping up in your mind, be gentle with yourself. Failure and mistakes are just training for future successes. Besides, would you be able to fully relish the joy of your successes if you had not experienced the exact opposite? It will never taste as good, I promise you. If you fail, it is very reassuring,

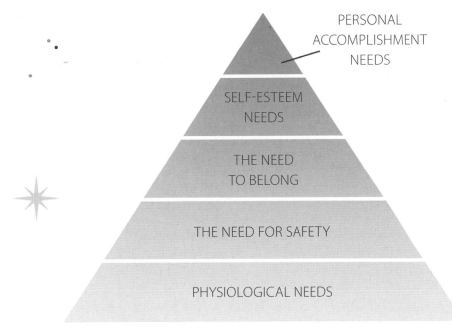

PERSONAL
ACCOMPLISHMENT
NEEDS

SELF-ESTEEM
NEEDS

THE NEED
TO BELONG

THE NEED FOR SAFETY

PHYSIOLOGICAL NEEDS

because this confirms that you are a human being in constant evolution. And that is perfectly perfect!

To help put yourself and your life into perspective, start a **bad mood book** – ideally black – where you list everything you dislike and find negative. This is your outlet for letting off steam – hold nothing back and feel free to sprinkle it with swear words if you want to. For this to be beneficial, the only condition is that you never read it again! Make another book – preferably pink – your **good mood book**. Write down everything that brings you happiness, be it small, medium or great! This notebook will be full of positivity and you can read it as often as you like. Having filled many notebooks myself, I encourage you to reread your pink notebook whenever you feel the need.

🗨 Welcoming and managing your emotions

Emotion is an energy. If you try and repress it, this energy will express itself in physical form and will have a direct impact on your physical health. As an emotion is biological and only lasts a few minutes, it is the feelings associated with this emotion that will lengthen its duration and affect our health (be it mental, emotional, psychic or physical). Our brain instinctively protects us from things that endanger us. This is why, in the wake of an emotional shock, some of our emotions are immediately buried in our unconscious. When they resurface in our conscious mind, the effect can be very violent. This is why it is essential to identify, name and express our emotions. This is

DOMINO EFFECT

Our emotions trigger chain reactions throughout our body. Each one takes place in four stages.

CHARGING:
emotions are charged by our mind (our thoughts) or our five senses. The part of our brain known as the thalamus receives an unusual signal. It reacts by sending a series of different orders to our body.

TENSION:
our body produces adrenaline and stimulates our sympathetic (adrenergic) nervous system. The direct consequence is mainly an increase in heart and respiration rate and in muscle tone.

OFF-LOADING:
this is the explosive phase which degenerates into anger, tears or anxiety attacks, as well as excitement and delight in the more positive cases. It is the off-loading of stored burdens and tensions.

RECOVERY:
our body must regenerate to find equilibrium once again. During this phase, we gather our strength, fulfil our needs and return serenely to a state of calm.

how we considerably reduce their impact, because we are no longer 'reacting' but 'responding'.

To help you with this, I recommend that you write down in a notebook (whatever colour you like) any situations which generate emotions in you. Ideally, perform this exercise at the same time as you are experiencing the emotion. Describe the emotion precisely, making note of the impact you observe. Writing will help your awareness. Then stand in front of a mirror. Look at yourself and smile for at least 3 minutes. Trust me, try it, even if you don't feel like it! The endorphins released by smiling will make you more objective about the situation that triggered your emotion and will help to calm your inner turmoil.

🌑 Opening up to the paranormal

Who better than a child to believe in the power of magic? You will almost certainly say you are too old for that, but what about your **inner child**? The inner child is an important concept in contemporary psychology according to Carl Gustav Jung, and it is closely linked to the archetype of the child (*puer aeternus*, in Latin). However old we are, we have a childlike part inside that has been with us since we were very young. Well hidden behind our serious adult mask, it seeks to be acknowledged and liberated.

I would like you to try and reconnect with your inner child so you can gently rediscover that capacity for wonder. Without judgement or constraint, think back to what you enjoyed doing most when you were a child. Were you an extrovert or an introvert? Very sociable or with your head in the clouds? Did you prefer sporty, creative or practical activities? Did you like trips to the forest or to the library? What is it that prevents you from really participating in these activities or expressing these personality traits as an adult? Is it fear of the judgement of others, social pressure or mental overload? Let your inner child's deepest aspirations shine through authentically because it wants nothing more! However, remember that it is all a balancing act. Don't go to the other extreme by shirking your responsibilities, obligations and objectives. I like to say that you can do serious things without having to take yourself seriously.

When I went back to singing in the bath, dancing while doing the housework, laughing without restraint and also spontaneously interacting with children that I met, I immediately reconnected with the little girl I used to be. I hope you have an equally powerful reconnection however you achieve it.

My advice, if you want to take concrete steps to open yourself up to the paranormal, is to start with the world of magic. Go to a magic show or watch videos of magic tricks. This might seem trivial, but for the more Cartesian among us, it is not. Let your mind go with it, and above all don't look for 'the trick'. Let yourself be swept along by the fact that you do not understand or control events. You are at the very start of the long exploratory path of synchronicity.

LIMITING BELIEFS AND FALSE IDEAS ABOUT SYNCHRONICITY

A few clicks on the internet are all it takes to discover a multitude of limiting beliefs and misconceptions about synchronicity.

Let us take a good look at four popular misconceptions, or as I refer to them below, 'received ideas'.

RECEIVED IDEA N° 1

This phenomenon has not been scientifically proven, so it is worthless.

True and false !
Does this seem a bit of a glib answer? I have heard this misconception stated on several occasions, and this is my response each time. It is a fact that the theory of synchronicity is still considered a 'pseudo-science'. But even if we do not learn it in the school classroom, even if it is often perceived as mysterious and not believed by everyone, why say that it is worthless? In my opinion, you first need to try a dish in order to say that you don't like it.

So, if one day it is proven to me that none of it exists, I will continue to live my life in the same way. In my eyes, the main thing is the result. The benefits obtained, such as the happiness, joy and positivity in my life and that of others, are too important not to want to safeguard them.

RECEIVED IDEA N° 2

You need to be blessed with exceptional powers to experience synchronicity.

Untrue!

And yet, many fatalists casually claim that you either have this gift or you do not. But in my opinion, this is really not the case! The phenomenon of synchronicity is not reserved for an elite or for those people with an insight into the strange and unusual.

We are all born with gifts and abilities, but the level of our natural abilities are not necessarily equal. Some people, who are naturally more observant, positive, alert and open, will have greater abilities than others. But plenty can still be achieved, it may just take more practise. And, if you are someone for whom it does not come naturally, you may even find your experience of the phenomenon of synchronicity is more intense than the experience of those for whom it does.

In the vast field of personal growth and holistic wellness, there are no 'chosen ones' – people with powers that are impossible to achieve or exceptional beings simply there to be idolized. We are all extraordinarily ordinary, because we have incarnated to evolve on all levels of our lives (personal, spiritual, professional, etc.) via paths and senses of purpose that can differ hugely.

RECEIVED IDEA N° 3

Synchronicities are exclusively positive.

Untrue!

Synchronicities do not exclusively herald good news. A series of difficult events sometimes prove to be cyclical nightmares that cause major upset and frustration. Although they are much less pleasant, glamorous and illuminating to share, they are real. In my opinion, it is worth consciously acknowledging and welcoming them, because these things do not happen by chance.

This calls to mind an anecdote from one of my coachees who held this belief, that is that the phenomenon of synchronicities was only positive. She had even brought me several articles from therapists and wellness professionals as proof of this fact. A few weeks later, however, she was astonished to find that after failing to get a series of jobs due to 'negative' synchronicities, her life had changed. As a result of these synchronicities, she realised that she had been in denial and moved into a new area of work. In a kind of reverse providence, a month later she got a great job. As she was in doubt, she asked the Universe for two signs to confirm that it was the right choice and an area in which she could thrive. She was amazed to discover how quickly life could respond!

RECEIVED IDEA N° 4

It won't work if you don't believe in it.

Untrue!

Well, partially at least, because conscious will is essential. Even if synchronicities exist, if we don't want to acknowledge their presence in our lives, we will never see them. It is as if we were wearing glasses with anti-synchronicity filters. The phenomenon may be present and possible to perceive, but if our personal filters (such as limiting beliefs, education and religion) prevent us from seeing it, nothing is going to happen. This is why it is important to open yourself up to new sensations, innovative concepts and new ways of thinking by accepting the fact that this phenomenon may be possible and real. Make yourself fully available internally and be ready to question the way you see the world. The power of synchronicity is intimately linked to the power of intention. As author Marcel Proust wrote in *Rembrance of Things Past*, 'The true voyage of discovery consists not in seeking new landscapes, but in having new eyes.'

IN SUMMARY

To experience synchronicities in an optimum fashion, it is important to have a positive state of mind, to be balanced, to fulfil your own needs, to manage your emotions and to be open to paranormal phenomena.

Not everything that is not (yet!) scientifically proven should be dismissed. To come to your own opinion, you need to test and experiment.

The phenomenon of synchronicity is not reserved for an elite or people with an insight into the strange and unusual.

Synchronicities do not exclusively herald good news. On the other hand, they can help us to step outside of our comfort zone or a phase of denial so we can undergo a positive evolution as we travel on our life's path. Our personal filters (such as limiting beliefs, education and religion) sometimes render us blind to synchronicities.

A DAY LIVING IN SYNCHRONICITY

In the third section of this book, I invite you to spend a day in a way totally unlike any that you have spent previously, a day dedicated to experiencing synchronicity. The next 24 hours will be punctuated by five important moments: the morning (to appreciate it), lunchtime (to observe it), teatime (to go into more depth about it), the evening (to interpret it) and the night (to attract it to you). All that I ask of you is that before you embark on this day, you set aside the limits of your mind and be prepared to do things that may appear irrational.

01

07:00
THE MORNING: APPRECIATING SYNCHRONICITY

Good morning – it's time to wake up to synchronicity! Welcome, I am delighted to introduce you to this new world. You have a beautiful journey ahead of you. To begin with, I suggest that you (un)settle yourself and make sure that you are anchored.

WHAT IS BEING ANCHORED?

Being anchored, or grounded, is:
- being attached to the Earth;
- living consciously, in the present moment;
- being perfectly connected to cosmic and telluric energies;
- being fully aware of being in your rightful place at every moment of your life.

I believe in successive lives and incarnations, and that our soul can only inhabit one vehicle, our body. It is therefore important that we protect, maintain and preserve it. From an energy perspective, anchoring helps us to detach our minds and use our visceral powers to become fully aware of our body and feel safe within it. Being grounded is also about accepting your body in order to engage serenely in your life.

Someone who is properly grounded holds themselves naturally upright, with pride and dignity. They accept life without resisting it. Like a tree that extends its branches towards the sky, such a person keeps themselves open to the world and does not get lost in their own thoughts, because they have deep roots. Using another analogy from Mother Nature, anchoring allows us to transform ourselves into an flexible reed which, perfectly balanced with the wind, bends but never breaks.

I have discovered that it is sometimes irrational to avoid so many signs on the pretext of wanting to remain rational.
STÉPHANE ALLIX

FINDING YOUR ANCHOR POINT

The tree-rooting meditation is a meditative practice that will help you to anchor or ground yourself. But if meditative practice doesn't work for you, there are alternatives (see page 47).

1. Sit on a chair, back straight (without leaning against the chair back), legs uncrossed. Put your bare feet flat on the floor and place your palms on your thighs. Relax, close your eyes and focus on your breathing.

2. Then, at your own pace, move your attention down through your stomach, your hips and your legs and imagine big, long roots coming out of your feet. They penetrate deep into the ground to the centre of the Earth. Draw in as much light energy from there as you can before bringing it up through the roots, and back up through your body to the top of your skull. While remaining firmly rooted, a thread comes from your head and extends higher and higher beyond the clouds into the Universe so as to hook itself on to it, and that's it,

you are anchored. What sensations are you experiencing? What do you feel? Pay close attention to the emotions running through you. Capture the most positive ones and form them into a point of light, then anchor it deeply to your heart. Your roots will be invisible, but you will be able to connect with their energy at any time through this anchor point.

3. To come out of your meditative state, take three deep breaths. Then, at your own pace, open your eyes and regain awareness of your whole body.

In general, it takes time to become properly anchored and grounded. The first few times, your grounding may be fragile and you will have to persevere in order to develop and strengthen it. I advise you to practise it daily and whenever you feel the need. This way you can quickly reconnect with your personal anchor point.

WE ARE ALL CONNECTED

We are connected to Mother Earth and the energies around us, but that is not all! Even if we don't know each other, I have a deep conviction that we are all connected to each other. The principle of **social synchronicity** is rooted in collective memory. This inexhaustible database of our evolution, like the links of a chain, means that each living being is attached to others, through its vibratory energy (mental, emotional, spiritual and physical). Each of us has our own place and our own importance in this living circle. The **story of the hundreth monkey** provides a perfect illustration of this idea.

South African biologist and zoologist, Lyall Watson (1939-2008), described in his book *Lifetide* how on the small island of Kōjima, Japan, scientists had been studying Japanese macaques (*Macaca fuscata*). A female macaque developed the habit of wetting and washing the sweet potatoes that had been dropped in the sand before she ate them. Between 1952 and 1958, the first monkeys to imitate the female's behaviour were the youngest monkeys on the island. As time went by, scientists noticed the habit becoming more and more widespread, particularly among a large number of females. The most reluctant to change their behaviour were the older male macaques. Years passed, until in the autumn of 1958, the group of sweet-potato washing monkeys grew to about 100 individuals, and it is then that, according to Watson, the scientists noticed a most extraordinary phenomenon. Symbolically, it is said that when the hundredth monkey started this new behaviour, the entire macaque community of Kōjima began to adopt this technique. Even more extraordinarily, it seems this new behaviour had been emulated among monkeys living on other islands, including the Takasaki colony (even though they were more than 13 hours away by train!).

Based on this observation, Watson initiated the 'critical mass' thesis, that is that once the sweet-potato washers reached critical mass, for argument's sake 100, then their behaviour changed the behaviour of the whole group on Kōjima. The addition of psychic energy from this hundredth monkey is thought to have created an unexpected cultural revolution.

What a beautiful message from nature! If we transpose this theory to humans, in a social context, imagine the power of its resonance! When a certain number of people reach a certain level of consciousness, it can then be transmitted from one mind to another. Although the exact number affected by this change varies, the phenomenon remains the same.

ANCHORING
ALTERNATIVES TO MEDITATION

If you are not receptive to meditative practice, here are various alternatives that will help you to anchor yourself in order to (re-)establish and maintain your dynamic equilibrium:

———

Take part in sports activities that put your feet into action (walking, running, cycling, etc.), taking the time to give yourself a good stretch.

———

Dance or sing, or just listen to music.

———

Enjoy nature by going for a walk in a park or forest, or by swimming in a lake.

———

Spend time with the people and animals you feel comfortable with.

———

Do some gardening, pottery or any other activity that requires you to get your hands dirty.

———

Practise martial arts;
get a massage.

———

Walk barefoot whenever it is possible, focusing on the contact of your feet with the ground.

———

Have fun and laugh as much as you can!

MORPHIC RESONANCE

Have you heard of morphic resonance? This concept, which is also known as the morphic field or morphogenetic field, demonstrates that matter is not necessarily required in order to contain energy or information. According to British research bio-chemist, physiologist and parapsychologist, Rupert Sheldrake, morphic resonance is a determining factor in the behaviour of living beings, particularly when they inherit habits linked to their species, and their actions influence their fields of form. Fields of form, which are also referred to as morphogenetic fields and morphic resonances (or fields), contain non-mate-rial energy (or information). For example, these fields are not composed of electrons. In this theory, Rupert Sheldrake makes an analogy with the physical notion of the force field (a set of parameters describing the structure of the potential energy of a system of particles such as atoms).

Some people speak of a 'magic formula' combining the law of resonance and the force of egregores (a group spirit consti-tuting the energy, intentions and desires of several people united in the same goal). This 'magic formula' would be the result of the square root of 1% of the population. For 1 million people, it would therefore only take 10,000 people for change to occur spontaneously. Interesting, isn't it?

THE FEATHER EXPERIMENT

To appreciate your interconnection with other living beings and experience the power of synchronicity, I suggest you try the feather experiment.

First of all, make sure you are well anchored, using the tree-rooting meditation if necessary (see page 45). Making yourself comfortable, sitting or lying down, close your eyes and visualise a feather. Observe it in great detail for at least a minute. You should, for example, be able to answer the following questions: What shape is it? What is its composition? Its colour? Its smell? Its texture? How much does it weigh?

When you have visualised your feather, surround it with a golden circle of light. Then open your eyes and resume normal activity without thinking any more about it. With the feather now in your mind, it is no longer your conscious that is at play, but the unconscious (yours and the collective), working to bring this feather to you in the present moment.

I have done this exercise several times. Each time, I am surprised at how quickly the Universe responds to my thoughts. I remember once, a few hours later, I passed a little dog in the street with a coat decorated with feathers. A few metres further on, in front of a shop, a child was telling her mother that she had to buy a 'quill' pen for school and not a ballpoint, as her mother was suggesting.

MY TIPS

1

If you prefer, choose any small object of your choice instead (a pebble, a pencil or a pair of glasses, for example).

2

The most difficult part of this experiment is to forget about the chosen object. The more you let your thoughts go, the more you will allow the Universe to get on with its work until it becomes a reality in your life. So stop thinking about the result and let life bring you the information.

YOUR WORLD MAP, YOUR FRAME OF REFERENCE

Neuro-linguistic programming, or NLP, is a novel approach to the way humans function, founded by Americans Richard Bandler (mathematician and Gestalt therapy practitioner) and John Grinder (linguist and psychologist) in the 1970s. NLP seeks to understand our personal and interpersonal structure. It is based on the observation of multiple human behaviours and particularly focuses on the 'how' rather than the 'why'.

NLP makes use of ten presuppositions, one of which resonates with the phenomenon of synchronicity: our perception of reality is not reality itself. Thus, for the Polish-American philosopher and scientist Alfred Korzybski (1879-1950), 'A map is not the territory it represents.' Indeed, as Umberto Eco, Italian writer and philosopher (1932-2016) wrote, 'We read the map and we think we read the order of the world. But the map is not the land, it is simply a construct of our mind. There is no guarantee that the map is accurate.'

Our perception of reality corresponds to our personal world map (our frame of reference).

Our world map influences our choices, our desires and our perceptions. This personal map gives a partial, and often erroneous representation of the full territory.

Since our reality of things is not the 'true reality', and we act according to a representation of it, two people will never perceive the world in the same way. This is why it is essential, if you want to experience synchronicity properly, to use your own personal experience and frame of reference as a foundation, remembering that our perception is totally subjective. A synchronicity may have a particular meaning for one person and at the same time have no significance at all for another. There is no good or bad map, but the more open, observant, optimistic and curious you are, the bigger your map will be.

It is important to be aware that everyone has their own map of reality. So what is true for one person may not be so for another, as we are all different and complementary. The only thing that is almost certainly true is that they are probably both right!

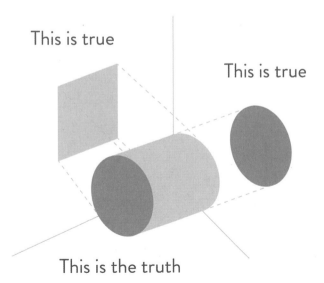

Every man takes the limits of his own field of vision for the limits of the world.
Arthur Schopenhauer

TRANSFORMING YOUR LIMITING BELIEFS

Although we are connected and complementary, we are none the less very different from each other, particularly in the way we think and our perception of reality.

With so much information constantly assaulting our senses, our brain cannot keep up. As it cannot possibly deal with all the pieces of information it receives every second, our conscious mind must sort them to filter out those that are the best and most useful. As the years pass and life experiences accumulate, our filters develop and grow stronger. This is why young people, without much life experience, are able to accept a new idea with much greater speed and ease. But even if you have 40, 50, 60 or more years of life behind you, don't imagine this to be impossible! You will just need to work a little harder to transform or replace your filters.

Our beliefs influence and stimulate the development of our filters. They validate our internal concepts and authorise the actions that arise from them. I distinguish between two types of beliefs: those that help and those that limit. The first provide a positive structure and bring us meaning and happiness. The second, however, relate to what we don't know (ignorance, doubt, etc.) and limit our field of action (low self-esteem, etc.). They are sometimes a source of discomfort and prevent us from being ourselves. As you will have realised, as our day progresses into lunchtime, we are going to focus on your limiting beliefs, in order to appreciate synchronicities at their full value.

ADOPTING ANOTHER POINT OF VIEW

A common limiting belief is that unless I have A, I cannot do B which will make me happy. If this sounds familiar to you, I would suggest turning this around to say, 'I want to be happy so I will do B, and in order to do so, I will do everything I can to obtain A.'

RECIPE FOR FLIPPING YOUR BELIEFS LIKE PANCAKES

Ingredients:
- ☀ A ladle of motivation
- ☀ Two pinches of courage
- ☀ Three large spoonfuls of trust
- ☀ A cup of innovation and openness

1. List all the beliefs that you have on the subject of synchronicity. For example: I am not capable of seeing synchronicities; I will always have a problem picking up on them; if I manage to live with synchronicities, I am worried that...; everyone who lives with synchronicities is...

2. Divide your synchronicity-related beliefs into those that are helpful (positive) and those that are limiting (negative). Then, focus only on your limiting beliefs.

3. For each of them, answer the following three questions:
- What is your basis for thinking that?
- In your opinion, might other people think differently? Why?
- What do you think about it?

4. Follow this reflection by asking yourself about the impact of your thoughts:
- On your behavioural reactions. Is there one? If so, what is it?
- On your emotional reactions. Is there one? If so, what is it?

What, for you, are the consequences of your behavioural and/or emotional reactions?

5. Finally, what would you need to make the impact of your thoughts 100% positive? What could you specifically put into place in your life to achieve this? This might be some small form of action or something bigger, in several stages.

02

12:00
LUNCHTIME: OBSERVING SYNCHRONICITY

As midday approaches don't reach for your apron. A detective's trench coat would be more appropriate as you are going to transform your lunch into an investigation.

CONDUCTING THE INVESTIGATION

My private-eye metaphor might have brought a smile to your face. But if you look at it more closely, detectives have a tool that is indispensable to all apprentices to synchronicity: **a little notebook**.

I suggested on page 37 that you use a notebook to keep a track of your emotional responses to everyday situations. Likewise, even if you are blessed with the memory of an elephant, I advise you to keep a daily notebook to remind yourself of the synchronicities that will illuminate your path for several months or years. To start with, write down small details from your day-to-day life, even if they appear insignificant. Use a colour code to mark the power and intensity of each synchronous event (for example, red for 'major', orange for 'less significant' and green for 'minor'). You will notice over time that the more you record these experiences, the more the phenomenon becomes part of your life.

DEVELOPING YOUR 5 SENSES

Synchronicity is a muscle that you need to work for it to develop. This can be done in particular by the (re)connection and development of your five senses: taste, smell, sight, hearing and touch. The more powerful your senses, the more quickly you will pick up on synchronous events.

Our sense of **taste** allows us to distinguish between the five basic flavours and they are these: salty, bitter, sour, sweet and umami. Umami comes from the Japanese word for 'delicious' and it is the taste of monosodium glutamate.

The sense of **smell** has an incredible memory. Our oldest and most primitive sense, in present-day society it is often overlooked.

Our eyes are capable of perceiving 10 million different colours. This is something of which advertisers are well aware! As a consequence, our **sight** is subjected to almost constant overstimulation.

Our sense of **hearing** allows us to distinguish around 500,000 different tonalities.

Touch is the first sense to develop in utero. Babies are no more than a few weeks old when they develop this sense, two thirds of the way through the first trimester. And this is not just chance, because touch is essential for our survival. Aristotle wrote, 'The sense of touch is the sense without which living beings would die.'

5 SENSES IN 5 EXERCISES

Now you know about the most developed of your senses, I recommend that you start with some exercises for the ones for which you get your weakest results. This will increase your receptivity to synchronicities. Take your time, be patient and respect your personal rhythm so you can really explore your senses in depth.

🗨 Taste

I have, on several occasions, had the opportunity to participate in 'dinners in the dark', accompanied by both the visually impaired and people without disabilities. These unusual experiences have completely thrown my sense of taste into confusion. Once, I was absolutely certain I had eaten meat and yet it turned out that both the starter and the main course had been fish! If you can't get to one of these restaurants, try the experience at home, by organising one with family or friends. First of all, start with a mystery dessert, then on a different day select a main course, then go all out with a full dinner. Warn your guests, otherwise they might be a bit confused!

🗨 Smell

To develop the power of your nose, I recommend buying a new spice, an unfamiliar fruit or unusual vegetable each time you go shopping. Before eating, explore it exclusively with your nose. Close your eyes and consciously inhale its aroma. Do the same with perfumes, essential oils, herbs and flowers. This will allow you to add them more easily to your olfactory memory and your internal catalogue will then quickly gather new smells.

🌫 Sight

Be visually curious, wherever you are. On public transport, in waiting rooms, restaurants, classrooms or the open spaces of your office environment, look around you: at the objects, colours, shapes and also the people. How are they standing or sitting, how are they behaving, what are they doing and what are they wearing? Obviously you should be discreet and respectful: don't stare at anyone for any length of time!

Look for anything that is new in situations that are familiar to you, such as that alleyway you pass every day.

🌫 Hearing

Pay attention to others. Start with the people closest to you, then your friends, colleagues, right down to people you have just met on a night out or on the underground. To develop your hearing, you must practise active listening. Conceptualised by the American psychologist Carl Rogers (1902-1987), active listening consists of listening attentively to the person speaking. To do this, it is important to create a climate of trust, respect and empathy. Listen and let the other person express themselves completely freely. Do not intervene until

they have finished, do not interrupt or try to guide the conversation.

🌫 Touch

To increase your sense of touch, use your hands creatively. Painting, pottery, gardening or cooking will help you to develop your range of tactile sensations. To stimulate the receptors in the soles of your feet, spend as much time as possible walking barefoot. Another good exercise is to try alternating thermal sensations by alternating experiences of heat (bath, drink), warmth (shower, swimming pool) and cold (ice-cream, ice-cubes).

TEST YOURSELF!

It's time to take the senses test on pages 60 and 61. Complete each statement by choosing one of the options given below it, being completely honest and transparent with yourself to select the one that most applies to you. The results at the base of page 61 will reveal what your choices tell you about your senses: which are your most dominant senses and which are your weakest ones. You can keep a record of the exercises you undertake to develop your senses by filling in the journal layout on page 123.

SENSES TEST

I prefer...

A. Eating a delicious chocolate mousse or a tasty home-made pizza.

B. Walking in a field of lavender.

C. Going for a massage.

D. Watching the sun rising or setting.

E. Going to a concert or listening to music at home.

STATEMENT N° 2

When I am tired, I need to...

A. Use essential oils.

B. Do a revitalising face mask.

C. Lie down and watch a box set or something on TV.

D. Rest or meditate with some soft music.

E. Make and savour a vitamin-C packed smoothie.

STATEMENT N° 3

When I use my memory, I can easily remember...

A. Clothes that I have worn.

B. Interior décor, the people present or the colours of their outfits.

C. Words that I have said or have heard.

D. What I have eaten or the delicious smell of a bakery.

E. The general ambiance of a memory or the smell of a place.

If I hear 'Christmas', I immediately think of...

A. Seasonal song compilations or choirs.

B. Delicious family recipes.

C. Spiced tea or mulled wine drunk on the go.

D. Gifts to be wrapped and opened on Christmas day.

E. A Christmas tree twinkling with lights.

My 'Proust's madeleine' (something that inspires childhood memories) is...

A. My grandmother's voice or the children's happy babble on my birthday.

B. Modelling clay or play-dough.

C. My first love's body spray or the smell of the school glue sticks.

D. A slice of cake or a chocolate biscuit eaten at break time.

E. The stickers that the school teacher gave me for good work.

RESULTS

Statement 1. A: taste; B: smell; C: touch; D: sight; E: hearing.

Statement 2. A: smell; B: touch; C: sight; D: hearing; E: taste.

Statement 3. A: touch; B: sight; C: hearing; D: taste; E: smell.

Statement 4. A: hearing; B: taste; C: smell; D: touch; E: sight.

Statement 5. A: hearing; B: touch; C: smell; D: taste; E: sight.

TOTAL TASTE : _____ TOTAL SMELL : _____

TOTAL TOUCH : _____ TOTAL SIGHT : _____ TOTAL HEARING : _____

OPENING UP YOUR INTUITIVE CHANNEL

Our sixth sense is an interesting ally when it comes to successfully observing synchronicities and understanding their subtlety. The more down-to-earth among you are probably asking how to switch on their sixth sense. And yet, we all have the capacity to be intuitive. Like the power of synchronicity, it is a gift. As with any gift, we are not all born equal. Some of us may have to experiment more to discover and reveal it.

The term intuition comes from the Latin *intueri*, which means 'look inside'. Introspection and the connection with our internal world are therefore essential. But there is no such thing as a high-speed wi-fi connection to your soul. In fact, finding yourself alone with yourself requires you to cut yourself off from external stimuli so you can listen to what your body, your senses and your feelings are telling you. To achieve this, some people might like the idea of a walk in natural surroundings, others a relaxation session, some meditation time or listening to music.

INCREASING YOUR VIBRATORY RATE

Synchronicities call on 'subtle' energies – the higher your vibratory rate, the easier it will be for you to capture them and be a good natural 'receptor'. **Radiesthesia** is the ability to sense energy forces, especially from the human body, and each living being has an energy vibration frequency made up of a number of oscillations over a given unit of time. The vibratory rate is expressed in Bovis units (named after its inventor, Antoine Bovis, a practitioner of radiesthesia operating in the 1930s). In radiesthetics, we use a Bovis biometer and a pendulum or pendant to make the calculation.

Someone's vibratory rate depends on their level of consciousness, their energy level (the light that they give off), but also their spiritual level. The purer the four levels of consciousness (physical, mental, emotional and spiritual), the higher the vibratory level. The higher our vibratory level, the better we can protect ourselves from external energy aggressions. When we calculate the vibratory rate, we talk about three dimensions: physical, energetic and spiritual. Are you ready to conduct a quick experiment to test your vibratory rate? Grab a pendulum or pendant and turn to pages 64-65.

The intuitive mind is a sacred gift and the rational mind is a faithful servant. We have created a society that honours the servant and has forgotten the gift.
ALBERT EINSTEIN

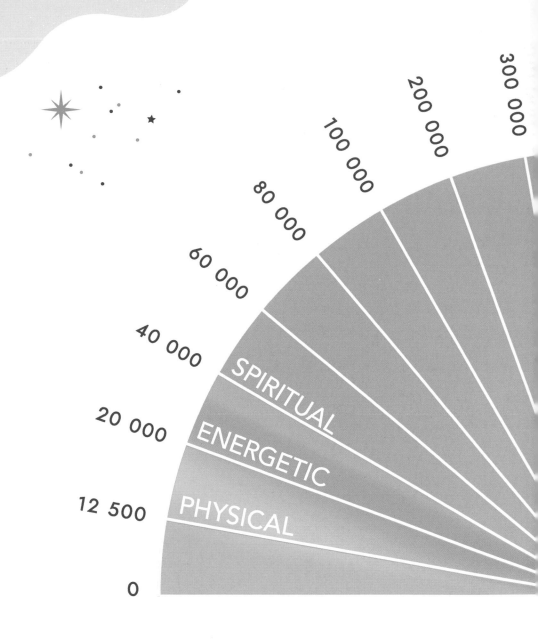

300 000

200 000

100 000

80 000

60 000

40 000

SPIRITUAL

20 000

ENERGETIC

12 500

PHYSICAL

0

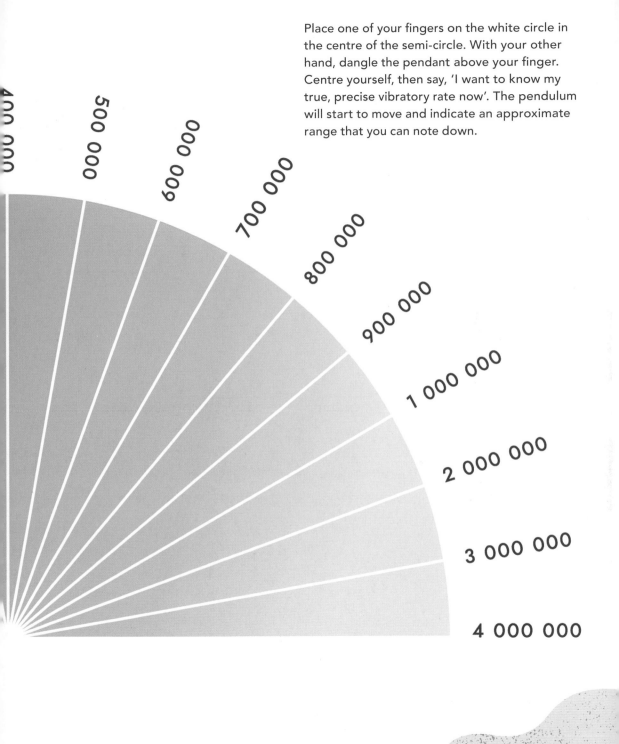

400 000

500 000

600 000

700 000

800 000

900 000

1 000 000

2 000 000

3 000 000

4 000 000

Place one of your fingers on the white circle in the centre of the semi-circle. With your other hand, dangle the pendant above your finger. Centre yourself, then say, 'I want to know my true, precise vibratory rate now'. The pendulum will start to move and indicate an approximate range that you can note down.

15 WAYS TO INCREASE YOUR VIBRATORY RATE NATURALLY:

1. Burn tree resin incense, such as benzoin, copal or storax.

2. Diffuse some incense, such as sage, basil or myrrh essential oil. Make sure it is pure, complete and organic.

3. Take some exercise (yoga or dance, etc.).

4. Reduce screentime and also protect yourself from potentially harmful 'waves' by staying away from wi-fi as much as you can.

5. Opt for local, organic and non-processed food as much as you can.

6. Drink at least 1.5 litres of filtered water a day.

7. Have fun and don't hold back on the laughter!

8. Spend time with the people and/or animals who make you feel good.

9. Listen to music and sing along without worrying about whether you are in tune.

10. Declutter your house, room by room.

11. Contemplate the present moment and enjoy it.

12. Keep faith and your positive mental state intact.

13. Let go of anything you cannot control.

14. Sunbathe, making sure you protect your skin with a good sun cream (basically, the higher the SPF, the better the protection).

15. Think positively and don't take life too seriously, because none of us are leaving it alive!

Being negative is to distance yourself from your happiness; being positive is to help it to grow.
David Cloutier

DEVELOPING AND TRAINING THE 6TH SENSE

To connect quickly with your intuition, I am going to suggest two exercises that you should do as often as you want.

☁ Think big

By saturating our field of vision, the predominant sense in today's society, we see things in a different way and so immediately change our perception of the world. To do this, look at something located in front of you.

Without moving your eyes from it, be visually attentive to everything happening around you. Try and go as far as possible to the right, the left, down and up, identifying shapes and colours without moving your eyes.

Then try to remain connected to the whole of your field of vision for at least 90 seconds. What do you feel?

Once you have shut off your mind, you can connect solely with the quiet internal voice of your intuition. The more you practise this exercise, the more you will see its impact on the way that you think and the power of your sixth sense.

☁ The pack of cards

For more intuition practice, you need a standard pack of cards. Shuffle the cards. Then ask the following question, 'Will the next card from the pack be red or black?' Before answering, close your eyes. Take three deep breaths and following your intuition, make your choice.

Turn over the card to find the result. Whether you are right or not, note it down in your little notebook, without judgement. Repeat several times, and above all, don't forget that the important thing is not to guess the right answer but to develop your sixth sense. As Winston Churchill wrote, 'Success is going from failure to failure with no loss of enthusiasm.' So, smile, you are on the right path!

TRAINING

Intuition is not a rational, 100%-reliable system. It is in your image, perfectly imperfect, and above all, human. Listen to your humanity and your feelings. Can you sense this person, this dish or this situation? Write your answers down in your little notebook. The more you exercise your intuition, the more refined it will become. You would not ask a young child to run as fast as a teenager, and the principle is the same here. Allow yourself the time for this essential, life-changing period of learning.

03

17:00
TEATIME: DEEPENING SYNCHRONICITY

After this mid-day observation phase, it is time to analyse this phenomenon in depth and have a play with it. Between sips of tea, you will discover its forms, its messages and its close link with numerology. It's teatime so get yourself a cup of your favourite brew, and don't forget the biscuits!

PLAYING WITH SYNCHRONICITY

Do you remember on page 37, we addressed the subject of your inner child? Playing is a natural, intuitive activity for children and has a major role in their daily lives. And, as you will discover, playing, having fun and enjoying yourself above everything else facilitates the experience of synchronicity.

Approach life as if it were a giant treasure hunt. In the eyes of children, synchronous events are simple pointers along the way. They can lead us to magnificent treasure. But watch out for anyone wanting to cheat or control the rules! You are a co-player in this game and not the single, unique games master. Margaret J. Wheatley and Myron Kellner-Rogers (authors of *A Simpler Way*) were quite right when they wrote, 'We could make our lives so much more interesting and develop so many new skills in ourselves, if only we tried to work with the unknowns inherent in the emergence of things rather than trying to plan the surprises in our lives.'

However, do not get stuck in the trap of obsessionally searching for signs, meanings and cerebral explanations. If you are pregnant, for example, you'll bump into many other women who are also pregnant, but that isn't necessarily an indicator that you made the right or the wrong decision about becoming a parent.

Yes, it is logical that you have lost your keys again if you keep telling yourself that you lose them all the time. This might seem obvious, but I have literally heard these very words. The Universe simply responds to the vibration that you give off. Sometimes that is all it means and you have to accept that. In an excessive search for signs, do not succumb to the temptation of superstition. Do

Synchronicity is a child playing, moving pieces over a chess board. From this side of reality, we see the pieces moving, but not the hand that moves them.
ROBERT MOSS

not fall into the trap of prediction. I was slyly drawn into this a few years ago, and I assure you that it will not do you any good.

Superstition and fortune-telling are psychically alienating, and when taken literally they disempower us. They disconnect us from our reality and lure us away from our path, sapping our energy and our confidence.

DISCOVERING THE DIFFERENT FORMS OF SYNCHRONICITY

Messages from the Universe can come in different forms: written (word, letter, number, etc.), via a visual medium (symbol, colour, material, etc.), oral (speech, radio or television programme), or by means of artistic expression (song, dance, painting, etc.). No one method is stronger than another. Its repetition and power depend on our capacity to receive the information that is meant for us, and in particular, our personal sensibility. Nineteenth-centrury poet Charles Baudelaire wrote, 'Despise the sensibility of nobody; each

man's sensibility is his genius.' We are constantly in metamorphosis and evolution, living through cycles of life. So it might be that at the present moment, you are more receptive to messages and in a few months' time, it will be mirror hours.

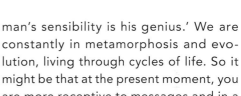 Messages
Whether they are written in a letter, a poem, a book, or on the street (chalk on a pavement, a graffiti tag), or heard in an advert or a song, or even as part of a conversation, messages can take a thousand and one forms. If they are meant for you, the Universe will ensure that you receive them. Remember, for Carl Gustav Jung, what is not brought to consciousness, comes to us as fate. Another theory is that these messages are responses to the mental projections of our subconscious needs.

The English politician Horace Walpole (1717-1797), having read the Persian fairy-tale of *The Travels and Adventures of the Three Princes of Serendip*, coined the word 'serendipity' and defined the principle as the ability to make an unexpected discovery by chance and to grasp its practical or scientific utility. Serendipity is closely linked to synchronicity. The theory set out by Horace Walpole lies in the importance of establishing your personal needs. Messages of synchronicity are mental projections of subconscious desires or traumas (abandonment, injustice, rejection, humiliation, betrayal) that still cause us to react.

We evolve in a society where on a day-to-day basis, from the moment we wake up, we step onto to a high-speed train of overstimulation and submersion in a never-ending stream of information. There are calls on our attention from all sides and this can exhaust us physically, mentally and emotionally, without us even realising. It is often the recurrence and not the synchronicity itself that is worthy of our attention. Luckily, the Universe has the patience of Job!

To open your intuitive channel to new messages, change the time you walk your dog, get off the underground one station early, stop at a bus station to complete your journey using a different means of transport, or push open the door of a shop you've never been in before. Seize the moment, then provoke and welcome the unexpected.

🍃 Slips of the tongue, Freudian slips, forgetfulness, mistakes and synchronicity

Acts or mistakes deemed slips of the tongue while speaking or writing have a crossover with synchronicity, as do Freudian slips or forgetfulness. They all reveal our unconscious desires. So if you are someone for whom such slips have always been a daily occurrence, don't blame it on inattention or lack of concentration. This form of natural clumsiness is a method the Universe uses to communicate with you and send through the (generally) gentle words it wants to pass on.

We are approximately 95% controlled by our unconscious mind (via our instinctive thoughts, words, gestures, reactions, etc.), and slips of the tongue and other oversights show the significant part it plays in our daily lives. For Freudian psychologists, these phenomena illustrate repression. In order to find expression, our repressed desires may manifest themselves in this roundabout way. Don't forget to write them down in your little notebook: take pleasure in unburdening yourself and find value in your weaknesses.

A BENEFICIAL TRICKSTER

The archetype of a trickster is present in almost every culture. Whether in the form of a streetwise kid, a gnome, a goblin or coyote, the little imp is a real chameleon. The character appears in different forms and loves chaos, because it provokes movement and change. According to Carl Gustav Jung, if this trickster appears to us (in synchronicities, dreams, nightmares, etc.), it is the symbol of a psychological transformation and response to a current need.

🐚 Mirror hours and numerology

As a numerologist and the author of *Guide d'introduction à la Numérologie* [translates to: *Introductory Guide to Numerology*], the extraordinary power of numbers has inspired me for many years. Immersed daily in their energy, I regularly answer questions about mirror hours.

What are mirror hours? They are those numbers that are doubled on the digital clock. For example, 07:07, 11:11 or 22:22. Not surprisingly then that they are sometimes also referred to as double or twin hours!

And what purpose do these mirror hours serve? There are many possible hypotheses, all linked to our subconscious. Time has been partitioned by humans. As a result, we may have been marked or traumatised by an event at a specific time and this reminder manifests itself regularly through our subconscious. Indeed, mirror hours are the source of many interpretations mixed with various beliefs (family, cultural, religious, and esoteric).

When we see a mirror hour, we may also think that:

☀ our guardian angel, guiding lights and other illuminating deities are communicating with us;

☀ a person (deceased or still incarnate) is thinking about us;

☀ it is an answer to a question we were asking ourselves;

☀ it reflects our thoughts, our emotional or physical state at that moment;

☀ it will bring us luck and we can make a wish.

I have given some interpretations for mirror numbers across the 24-hour day on the following pages. This is not an exhaustive list, the best thing to do is rely on your intuition and own senses.

00:00 HRS

KEY WORDS: DECISIONS, OPENNESS AND BEGINNINGS.

✳ You have a choice to make.

✳ Your thoughts are gaining momentum and things are starting to take shape in the direction you would like. Might you be thinking (too much) of others before thinking of yourself? Don't lose sight of your own personal well-being.

01:01 HRS

KEY WORDS: LOVE, INTROSPECTION AND MOVEMENT.

✳ Someone loves you.

✳ You are never alone. On the other hand, you may need to isolate yourself in order to (re)discover yourself more successfully.

✳ If you happen to catch sight of 01:01 while in a state of physical inactivity, this time reminds you that activity will be your salvation. Conversely, if you're already active, your initiative is to be congratulated.

02:02 HRS

KEY WORDS: SECRECY, OPPOSITION AND LAZINESS.

✳ Someone is hiding something from you.

✳ There is duality, antagonism or complementarity.

✳ You may currently think that you are in a situation from which there is no way out. Be more discerning.

✳ If you are passive, excessively withdrawn or spiritually lazy, it is time to come out of your hole and take action. If you are the opposite, you are on the right path.

03:03 HRS

KEY WORDS: CAUTION, INSPIRATION AND EXPRESSION.

✳ Someone's feelings towards you are not positive or caring. Beware!

✳ You have many ideas germinating at this moment in connection with your purpose in life.

✳ You know perfectly well what you want and what you no longer want in your life.

✳ You have good communication skills and you know how to make yourself heard. So enjoy your wonderful abilities!

04:04 HRS

KEY WORDS: ACTIVE LISTENING, NOVELTY AND LETTING GO.

✳ Pay close attention to a particular person, situation or event.

✳ You have everything you need to succeed. All that remains is to put it into practice.

✳ You are in spiritual progression, in a new cycle and/or a life change.

✳ Let go of anything that is no longer relevant so as to better welcome what is new.

05:05 HRS

KEY WORDS: CREATION, TRANSMISSION, ACTIVITY, VITALITY AND MAGNETISM.

✳ You have a definite sense of healing by the laying on of hands.

✳ You are the co-creator of your life, but be careful not to fall into being overly active, into 'doing'. Keep your feet on the ground, recentre yourself and take time to 'be'.

06:06 HRS

KEY WORDS: INTUITION, HARMONY, LOYALTY, WISDOM AND CHOICE.

✳ You learn very quickly and have the capacity to 'climb' spiritually. However, if this evolution is to be positive and beneficial, you need to be at peace with yourself.

✳ You have the power to express yourself, use it wisely.

07:07 HRS

KEY WORDS: AWARENESS, ASSOCIATION, EVOLUTION AND SPIRITUALITY.

✳ You know yourself very well. Share the knowledge gained through your experiences and awareness.

✳ You are on the right path to become an inspired and inspiring guide!

PREVIOUS LIVES

07:17 and 17:17 have strong resonances with your previous lives. It may be an action in the present (in your current life) that is based on a skill, or an experience in a past life (a life before your current one), or a connecting doorway opening into another dimension. If this resonates with you, explore this notion of memories and past lives.

08:08 HRS

KEY WORDS: LIBERATION, LAW, DISCIPLINE, ETHICS AND CONSCIENCE.

✹ You are advised to be wary of something.

✹ You are on the cusp of a great change in your life. Ensure you remain humble and candid, without boasting.

✹ Be who you are and not who others want you to be.

✹ Get closer to the people who trust in you.

HEALING

At 08:18 hrs and 18:18 hrs, detach yourself from certain 'toxic' people. Anchored in the present moment, you tune into the 'love' vibration.

09:09 HRS

KEY WORDS: COMPLEXITY, INNER LIFE, HUMANISM AND RESEARCH.

✹ A great friendship is beginning between you and another person.

✹ Do you know which way the wind is blowing in your life? Do you feel as if for every two steps forward you are taking one step back?

✹ Be careful and remain conscious of your limiting beliefs.

10:10 HRS

KEY WORDS: SELF-CONFIDENCE, ACHIEVEMENT, WEALTH, ELEVATION AND WORK.

✳ Even if you may think it, your life is not unhappy. You are the only one with the power to choose the right or wrong path.

✳ Opportunities for success are there and depend on nothing but your free will.

✳ Luck will smile on you if you open your mind to your intuition.

11:11 HRS

KEY WORDS: CHARISMA, VISIONARY ASPECT, NERVOUSNESS, THIRST FOR POWER AND REBELLION.

✳ Your love for someone is disproportionate and this is not fair on you. Be careful not to forget about yourself.

✳ You have everything you need for someone to love you.

✳ You have great innovative ideas, but your intuition is not yet fully developed. You are on the right track!

HOUR OF INSPIRATION

The time 11.11 hrs has inspired several artists, such as American director Darren Lynn Bousman, who released his film *11-11-11* on 11.11.11 (11th November 2011). This date was not chosen by chance since the plot of his film revolves round the '11.11' movement that brings together people obsessed by this double hour. In numerology, the number 11 is the first of the three 'master numbers' (the others are 22 and 33).

12:12 HRS

KEY WORDS: CLAIRVOYANCE, EVOLUTIONARY EVENT, KARMA AND VOLUNTARY RENUNCIATION.

☀ You are naturally gifted with good discernment.

☀ Congratulations, you are starting to become aware of your earthly trials, allowing your karmic baggage to be lightened.

13:13 HRS

KEY WORDS: DEATH AND RESURRECTION, CYCLICAL MUTATION AND A TASTE FOR CHANGE.

☀ Your wish or desire will come true.

☀ You are ready to begin a new phase and cycle in your life. So, don't hesitate to take action!

14:14 HRS

KEY WORDS: MOVEMENT, PROGRESS, INSTABILITY AND INVOLUTION.

☀ You are advised to give things another go.

☀ Pay attention to all your thoughts. If you want clarification on a particular subject, it should come through this channel.

☀ Don't dwell on your mistakes and failures.

15:15 HRS

KEY WORDS: PASSION, SEXUALITY, MAGNETISM, WILL AND REGRESSION.

☀ Your thoughts may be creating change in your life. If these changes are not wanted, stop yourself and transform your way of thinking.

☀ Be aware of your magnetism – you find it easy to attract people to you.

16:16 HRS

KEY WORDS: ARROGANCE, NEED FOR SOLITUDE, PURIFICATION, PRIDE AND ISOLATION.

✳ Let go of your thoughts and abandon your material concerns.

✳ If you are a believer, don't hesitate to ask for help (from angels, spirits, your guiding lights, etc.) with regard to taking care of a problem you are currently facing. Relax and let nature recharge your batteries.

17:17 HRS

KEY WORDS: WILL TO SUCCEED, CREATIVE FORCE, INTENSE ENERGY AND IMAGINATION.

✳ Congratulations, you are on the right path!

✳ Watch out for arguments with a lover.

✳ Be thankful and grateful. This will help you speed up the process of positive manifestations that you want in your life.

18:18 HRS

KEY WORDS: FAMILY DYNAMICS, HIGHER LOVE, RECEPTIVITY, MAGIC AND ILLUSION.

* Your wish will come true. Your hopes (especially emotional) for a better life are on the way to becoming reality.
* In terms of romance, a big thrill is coming your way!
* You are approaching the end of a significant cycle in your life.

SYMBOLISM OF 18

In numerology, the number 18 evokes femininity: it's the representation of the feminine in a couple and the symbolism of the sacred feminine in each of us. It is associated with the image of the Divine Mother, the moon and the Blessed Virgin Mary. The number 18 vibrates with the family unit. The people around you must become your priority.

19:19 HRS

KEY WORDS: UNIVERSAL LIGHT, TRANSCENDENT THOUGHT AND FRUITFUL ENERGY.

* You are asked to be patient.
* A new door is opening – it is the result of your deep desires. Visualise your wishes so that they come true more quickly.
* Let go of the old. The old will be replaced by the new in accordance with your aspirations.

20:20 HRS

KEY WORDS: SPEED, NEED FOR REASON, RAPID CYCLE OF HIGHS AND LOWS.

* The person you love is thinking about you.
* Perhaps you wish to be happier or in better health. If so, ask for help by opening yourself up to others so they can give you their advice.

21:21 HRS

KEY WORDS: ULTIMATE SUCCESS, DIVINE WISDOM, SYNTHESIS AND CORONATION.

* It is advisable for you to take the first step. Trust in yourself and go for it!
* You are on the cusp of achieving great things.
* Don't give up; subject your plans to the best possible analysis.

22:22 HRS

KEY WORDS: PRESTIGE AND RENOWN, SENSE OF MISSION AND GENIUS.

* You will receive a call from the person you love.

* If you feel forgotten or abandoned, know that you are loved. The Universe will never let you go.

* If you feel like you are stagnating at the moment, it is because certain things need to be in place before you can achieve the outcome you desire. As long as you hold on to your thoughts and continue to have faith, nothing can stop you from achieving your deepest desires.

FREQUENT MIRROR HOURS

Several surveys on the subject have indicated that 11:11 hrs and 22:22 hrs are the mirror hours that people catch sight of most frequently. Carried by the vibrations of these powerful master numbers, with the number 11 you reveal your magnetic energy, your creativity and the 'enhanced' part of yourself, and with the number 22, it is your energy for thinking outside of the box (for the well-being of everyone) that will be in the spotlight.

23:23 HRS

KEY WORDS: AGILITY, COURAGE, COMMUNICATION SKILLS, PROTECTION AND HERITAGE.

✳ The person you love needs you.

✳ Continue to collaborate with the Universe because everything is working out perfectly for you. You are already guaranteed a future full of the joy you seek.

✳ Don't let go, believe in yourself more than anything else.

STRANGE 137

Wolfgang Ernst Pauli, physicist and co-creator of the concept of synchronicity, was affected by the number 137 until his last breath. This number 137, also known as the 'fine structure constant', fascinated Pauli. He is quoted as saying, 'When I die, my first question to the devil will be, "What is the meaning of the fine structure constant?"'

A few days before his death, he was admitted to hospital and found himself in room 137. Pauli was certain the end was near, as he assured everyone who visited him. It has been said that Nobel Prize winning physicist Richard Feynman, an American scientist who, like Pauli, was awarded the Nobel Prize in Physics, suggested that all physicists put up a sign in front of their office or home with '137' on it, to honour Wolfgang Ernst Pauli and to acknowledge that it is impossible for anyone to know everything.

🐦 Repetitions

Arthur Koestler, Hungarian-born novelist and journalist (1905-1983), referring to the principle of repetition, spoke of 'puns of destiny'. This can be the repetition of events, things, words, numbers, colours, identical or similar symbols in time and/or space. The seriality of synchronicity is part of our secret garden. To us, it seems to be of great importance, but others may not see any interest in it at all.

When the same message comes to you more than twice in a short period of time (between several minutes and 48 hours maximum) it is of great importance. This repetition is a new opportunity for the Universe to attract your attention.

Even though we are still co-creators of our lives and bear total responsibility for our choices, I believe that there are milestones in our destiny which we are invited to pass. They are types of predefined waymarkers, and it is up to us to take the shortest or longest route to get to them. It may take a few weeks, several years, or it may never happen, but that does not detract from their existence.

To illustrate this, I have a very personal story to share with you. Meeting my husband in 2008 was not a coincidence at all. It was a genuine reunion for which there had been rehearsals of which we were not aware.

At the time of our first contact on the terrace of a Parisian café, we both had the impression that we already knew each other. This perception was so strong and unsettling that I felt compelled to investigate, even though I did not initially find him attractive. I didn't even think I would see him again. What a discovery it was when we realised that in the space of five years, we had had no fewer than seven opportunities to meet and chat to each other before D-day! From the office where he worked, which looked out on to the very park bench where I used to go with my kids after school, to visits to the same supermarket on the same days of the week, or sitting only a few seats apart at a concert venue. It was mind-blowing! These 'missed' opportunities were quite improbable and yet very real.

From that day on, we never left each other's sides. We were engaged within six months and we have been married now for over a decade. In that time we have learned that we have lived several significant past lives together. This could be one of the reasons why we have come together again in this lifetime. But the importance of these repetitions has played an essential role in our union. Without them, I am sure he would not be my husband today! Thank you, synchronicity!

☁ The symbolism of clouds

Clouds represent metamorphosis, change, elusiveness, reverie, but also dissimulation, secrecy and impermanence. Constantly changing, their shapes can reveal images with a strong symbolism. For example, you think of a loved one who has recently passed away and suddenly you see a heart-shaped cloud in the sky.

One of my client's had an experience so unique that she will not forget it in a hurry. After a reiki session, during which we had talked about children, she saw a cloud in the shape of a baby in the sky above Paris. A week later, she told me the good news. She was expecting her first child!

These signs and messages can appear in the sky, but they are also present on ground level too. When you go for a walk or a Sunday-afternoon stroll in the park, keep one eye on the stones and leaves around you. Their shape can carry a symbolic message.

☁ The symbolism of feathers

Feathers symbolise freedom, softness, grace and lightness. They are intimately linked to the majestic flight of birds to the heavens, the place where our loved ones rest in the light. I see feathers as a way for our guardian angels, our guiding lights or other deities we believe in to let us know they are there. By leaving feathers in our path, they invite us to take our time before continuing to write the next chapters of our lives.

At first glance, each feather looks the same and we don't pay any particular attention to it. But on closer inspection, we notice differences in colour, texture, material, weight and energy.

What differences do you see between the ten feathers on page 87? Do you think their colours have any influence? To explore this further, turn the page for Your Turn to Play.

YOUR TURN TO PLAY

To help shed more light on this symbolism, try the following exercise. Match the ten meanings (letters A to J) with the pictures of the ten feathers (numbered 1 to 10). You'll find the answers at the base of the opposite page.

USE YOUR INTUITION AND... NO CHEATING!

○ **A.** This feather tells you that an angel is nearby. It loves you, and is protecting and watching over you. It is currently putting everything into place in order to answer your requests (prayers, intentions).
Key words: hope, protection, peace, purification and spirituality.

○ **B.** This feather means that you will recover your health. Be reassured and serene. Draw on the energy of the Earth to replenish and regenerate you.
Key words: health, balance, stability, well-being and vitality.

○ **C.** This feather indicates that you will soon see light at the end of the tunnel. Hang on in there and take action to find solutions to the problems you are facing.
Key words: patience, confidence, courage, resilience and unblocking.

○ **D.** This feather reminds you that you are never alone. Do not hesitate to ask your angels and guides for help – even if they are not incarnate, they are always close to you.
Key words: sadness, malaise, crisis, difficult period and intense spiritual awakening.

○ **E.** This feather indicates that you are in the midst of a spiritual awakening. You are starting to develop your gifts into talents.
Key words: gifts, vitality, evolution, development and positive growth.

F. This feather confirms that you are on the right track, whatever choices you have made. Good for you!
Key words: intelligence, discernment, encouragement, positivism and success.

G. This feather symbolises love and relationships. You should be in for some pleasant emotional surprises in the near future.
Key words: sincere love, couple, family and birth.

H. This feather heralds a change in your life. The angels are surrounding you with luminous protection to ensure a smooth transition from the old to the new.
Key words: balance, harmony, renewal, protection and union.

I. This feather tells you not to give up. Happiness is not reserved for others. It will soon be knocking at your door, so be ready and stay positive.
Key words: motivation, happiness, joy, hope and a bright future.

J. This feather heralds a favourable outcome and a brighter future. You were suffering doubts, worry and turmoil, but that is all over now!
Key words: hope, balance, peace, light and serenity.

Answers: A-3, B-5, C-4, D-10, E-1, F-7, G-6, H-2, I-8 and J-9.

🐦 Animal symbolism

In addition to Carl Gustav Jung's anecdote about the scarab beetle (page 23) and Joseph Campbell's story of the praying mantis (page 24), it is important for me to share the symbolism of another 16 animals with you. Whether they cross your path or appear to you in a dream, animals always bring a particular message. They usually represent a situation, a problem or the answer to a problem.

4 BIRDS

The eagle informs you that something you have recently become aware of is life-saving. This powerful animal invites you to move to another level in order to increase your insight and connection with the invisible world.
Key words: divination, strength and prestige.

The owl symbolises truth, your truth. Wise and perceptive, it guides you towards the most authentic path possible. The owl allows you to uncover the liars who hide behind their social masks.
Key words: insight, intuition and truth.

The raven is the messenger of change. Considered a bird of ill omen, it is nevertheless the harbinger of the end of a cycle and an illuminated rebirth.
Key words: mourning, letting go and death.

The falcon has a particularly acute vision. With its sharp eyes, it invites you to look more closely at a situation, a person or a place.
Key words: vision, wisdom and protection.

4 REPTILES

The lizard brings your survival instinct to the fore. Don't be fooled by its size, because the lizard has a potent power of metamorphosis and regeneration. It means that good things are on their way.
Key words: renewal, rebirth and inner discovery.

The tortoise symbolises the Earth's energy. Its legendary calmness and patience gently connects you to ancient wisdom that will be to your benefit, especially during periods of chaos.
Key words: slowing down, stability and ancient wisdom.

The alligator invites you to reconnect with your primal instincts. Are your needs being sufficiently fulfilled and your values honoured? The alligator is there to remind you of this and help you to put things right.
Key words: hypersensitivity, protection and vital energy.

The snake informs you that it is important to reconnect with your deepest passions and aspirations. Ambivalent, intelligent and mysterious, this reptile is a powerful healer.
Key words: ambivalence, health and renewal.

The dragonfly is the messenger of protection. Although you may sometimes doubt it, it reminds you that you are never alone. The dragonfly confirms that you are on the right path to positive evolution.
Key words: self-confidence, protection and maturity.

The butterfly symbolises the desire for change, the need for freedom and lightness. Follow the energy of the butterfly, which is conducive to taking a step back and reconsidering things in a beneficial way.
Key words: transformation, personal growth and adaptation.

The ladybird brings luck and attracts riches (financial, material and sentimental). The ladybird invites you to develop your vulnerability and gratitude towards yourself and those around you.
Key words: luck, *joie de vivre* and wealth.

The spider is a powerful symbol of connection. Whether intellectual or relational, links are at the heart of the spider's message. It advises you to take action if you want to fulfil your deepest aspirations.
Key words: feminine energy, spirituality and creativity.

On the journey of shamanism with the Foundation for Shamanic Studies (founded in 1979 by Michael Harner), I must respect non-appropriation of other cultures in my practice. This is why I will never talk to you of totem animals. In my view, this subject is not a game or a superficial pseudo-trend. For me, the power animals that surround me, guide me and help me on my way, are much more than fashionable, stereotypical symbols. However, if the subject of totem animals calls to you and resonates particularly with you, you might like to study in more depth the writings and shamans of indigenous, Amerindian and African cultures. They constitute an infinite source of ancestral knowledge.

The lion triggers your feline instinct. Gifted with great power, the lion reminds you that, to develop greater stability and a more solid anchor, you must show courage in the situation in which you currently find yourself.
Key words: justice, courage and solidity.

The panther is a guardian of knowledge and human beings. It is a protector, and watches over you to make sure you do not stray too far from your life's path. The panther tests the limits of your independence, your strength and your flexibility.
Key words: benevolence, mysticism and motherhood.

The lynx is one of the powerful symbols of secrets and mystery. It says little, but sees everything. The lynx symbolises that you cannot be deceived, lied to or tricked. So, keep your mouth closed tight and your eyes wide open!
Key words: silence, observation and clairvoyance.

The wildcat has charisma and a sacred aura. The audacious, purposeful wildcat is very resourceful. As it always achieves its aims, this highly intelligent animal will help you out of even the most difficult of situations.
Key words: ingenuity, observation and determination.

03

20:00
THE EVENING: INTERPRETING SYNCHRONICITY

You have now been experiencing the power of synchronicity since breakfast-time, 13 hours ago. To travel still further, I suggest you sit down over supper and learn to interpret its signs and messages. On the menu, the art of divination to whet your appetite. The main course will pay homage to the modified state of consciousness. Finally, to finish on a sweet note, you will taste the delicious magic of the present instant. Are you ready?

THE ART OF DIVINATION IN THE SERVICE OF YOUR LIFE

The idea that the vibratory trace, the symbolic message and specific information about a future event can be already received, understood and dealt with in the present moment by our intelligence (bodily, emotional or analytical) seems crazy. But it is very real. Dr. Dean Radin, Chief Scientist of the Institute of Noetic Sciences, has demonstrated in his study 'Electrophysiological Evidence of Intuition. Part 1: The Surprising Role of the Heart',

that we can feel the anticipatory effects of a bodily stimulus about 5 seconds before the arrival of a fear-inducing image compared to a conventional one. When heart rate variability is observed, these effects even occur about 1 second more quickly. He therefore concluded that the more engaged and involved we are in this future event, the faster we will react to it.

In life, I believe that if you lose the magic, you lose the wonder, the freshness of discovery, the motivation and validity of spontaneity. As soon as we are no longer natural and authentic, we cut ourselves off from our emotions and therefore from the potential surprises of the Universe. When an event becomes routine and habitual, we feel less concerned and involved in it, because our curiosity is no longer stimulated. The novelty effect has worn off. This experience will therefore have less impact on our lives, both in the present and in the future.

Returning again to Carl Gustav Jung, he found that emotional investment was an

The holy sages were able to survey all the confused diversities under heaven. They observed forms and phenomena and made representations of things and their attributes. They were called: the images.

LE YI KING

extremely important factor in his parapsychological experiments on the subject. According to Jung, 'Our psychophysiological system responds to stimuli apprehended intuitively in the same way as it does to stimuli that are actually present.' The same processes are applied, regardless of the object's place in the course of time.

This capacity for perception that transcends time is a form of physiological foresight that is akin to a physical presentiment rather than mental precognition. Our attention span has the ability to extend beyond the present moment, so our autonomic nervous system is already 'responding' in advance to events that have not yet happened, but which it anticipates in order to better prepare for them. It is an indispensable tool for developing our synchronistic intuition, our mind being much larger and broader than our brain.

DISCOVERING THE I CHING, ORACLES AND BIBLIOMANCY

The Chinese divinatory text of I Ching (易经 in simplified Chinese and 易經 in traditional Chinese) is also known as the 'Yellow Book, the Book of Changes, Transformations, Mutations or Metamorphoses'.

I CHING: A SHORT HISTORY

Legend tells that around 5,000 years ago, while meditating near a river, a strange creature (a mixture of a tortoise, horse and dragon) appeared to the Chinese emperor Fu Xi from out of the water. Symbols appeared to form naturally on the animal's scales, which the emperor saw as a series of trigrams, and by associating them he claimed that he was able to bring together the sum of all knowledge.

Considered to be one of six sacred books, the I Ching book was about divination, but it can also be considered a philosophical work. Originally, this method of reading the future involved a technique of listening to the Earth used in conjunction with Feng Shui. The first users of I Ching can be traced back to between 1000 and 500 BC. They were priests of the feudal period under the third Chinese dynasty, the Zhou. In the pages that follow, we'll take a look at how the I Ching is used, as well as two other popular methods of divination: oracles and bibliomancy.

The I Ching hexagrams

The I Ching comprises a set of 64 hexagrams, which represent all possible combinations of a stack of six solid or broken horizontal lines. To form the hexagrams, 50 small bamboo slips (known traditionally as yarrow stalks) are provided with the Book of Changes. To use the I Ching, you start by setting one stalk aside before randomly sorting the remaining stalks. From this point on, there are various methods. The most well-known starts by making a movement with the thumb of the left hand to divide the pile of the remaining 49 stalks in half. You now have two unequal piles. Take one stalk from the right-hand pile and place it between your little finger and ring finger of your left hand. Holding the stalk between these two fingers, then take hold of the left-hand pile in your left hand. Then, using your right hand, remove the stalks in groups of four, until a total of four stalks or fewer remain in your hand. Place the remaining stalks between your ring finger and middle finger of your left hand.

According to the Swiss psychotherapist and author, Verena Kast, 'the question asked by the I Ching is not what is to be done, but in which of life's power relationships our action is located'. I find this describes perfectly how this Taoist oracle works. With the I Ching, don't expect a predictive, directive message. Each hexagram reveals the archetypal structure that is acting in the present moment. It guides us through each issue in order to make an enlightened choice, consistent with this structure, to follow the natural flow of life.

However, Carl Gustav Jung warns us about the possible excesses and abuses of divinatory methods, 'The I Ching does not offer itself with proof or results, it does not vaunt itself for its own sake, but for lovers of self-knowledge, of wisdom in thought and action.' So if we seek to take control, to develop our power by force and to use only our mind, these precious tools will be of no use at all. The oracles and the I Ching can only be questioned with benevolence, openness, respect and by letting go.

SLICE OF LIFE

I never thought I was predestined to practise the I Ching, but that was before finding out more about the power of synchronicity!

Three events turned me towards this mysterious divinatory art. During a meditative experience in late 2012, I saw myself opening a yellow book with wooden chopsticks. The first person I discussed it with was of Chinese origin. She smiled and briefly explained what the I Ching was. A few months later, I trained to become a facilitator for the game of Tao Long. This game of personal development is a fun educational tool for enhancing cooperation. During my training, we learned about the I Ching. Then, in the summer of 2013, my grandmother passed away. When, with respect and kindness, our family gathered to clear out her flat, I felt her presence strongly. My aunt took from the hands of another family member a bundle of dusty wooden sticks and an ancient yellow book in which my grandmother had left several small pieces of paper with written notes and calculations, and passed it me saying with certainty, 'That is for Anne-Sophie, Grandma would have wanted her to have it.' My husband and I were flabbergasted for it was, of course, the I Ching. Even today, I still have all my grandmother's notes and I use her set.

Oracles

The current trend is towards oracles. But do you know precisely what they are? From the Latin *orare*, meaning 'to speak', the term oracle has a divine connotation. It is a channel the gods use to express themselves. From time immemorial, human beings have deciphered the messages of invisible beings and higher powers through oracles. Some people with naturally developed sensibility and intuition use oracles to guide those who consult them. You may be familiar with the Oracle of Delphi, famous from Greek mythology that is said to have passed on the word of the Olympian gods. The prophetess of Delphi, the Pythia, was the only person able to channel the oracle, ans the questions that were put to it.

Nowadays, there are many different types of oracle cards. You are sure to find a deck that suits you. Be guided to the right set for you on the basis of the themes, the titles, the number of cards and the inspiring messages given. Unlike tarot, there are no rules that you need to know or principles that must be respected with this divinatory tool. Each oracle has different vibrations and different suggestions in terms of the way they should be drawn, but there is no hierarchy between the cards. It is up to you to pick one or several at a time.

ORACLE OF THE RISING SUN

Inari, the god of rice, the harvest and fertility, is worshipped throughout Japan, where there are more than 30,000 shrines dedicated to him. This deity is represented by the fox who delivers the oracle (in the form of initiation rites).

🕮 Bibliomancy

The word bibliomancy comes from the Greek βιβλια (*biblia*) meaning 'book' and μαντεια (*manteia*), 'divination', and is a divinatory method using written material. This method dates back to the times when writing was done on papyrus.

It is very easy to do. All you need is a book, be it a reference guide, a novel, a sacred book, an essay, a collection of poetry or even a dictionary. Then close your eyes and take three deep breaths. Think about your problem or state your question out loud to your guiding lights, to God or simply to the book in front of you. Then, when you feel ready to find the answer you need, open your book. Without looking, point to a word or phrase, following your intuition. Open your eyes to discover the message. As you read it, be aware of your initial thoughts and feelings. Does it resonate with you?

Arthur Koestler, to whom we were first introduced on page 83, spoke of the 'library angel'. According to him, a benevolent and studious spirit is to be found in certain libraries or bookshops. It is the source of the books that fall open at our feet on a page that brings us an important message. This reminds me of when, in the middle of writing one of my books, I was looking for a book I needed to refer to in my large personal library, which was far too overcrowded for my husband's taste! Needless to say, it could not be found. A few months later, as I was putting the finishing touches to the book, it took me no more than 5 minutes to lay my hands on it! It had slipped inside another one! When I reread it, I realised that it would not have been any use to me at all. It would have been a waste of time. Many thanks to my library angel for this helping hand!

By way of a contrasting experience, a few years ago, during my first visit to an esoteric Parisian bookshop, something striking occurred. As I walked past a glass cabinet displaying clocks, several of them began to spin and one of them even fell off its shelf. The saleswoman explained that it was meant for me as a book fell at our feet. Its title was directly related to intuition and taking your destiny in hand. I cannot deny that I was a little spooked at the time, even though I laughed it off with the saleswoman. I did not choose the book, the clock did, and it was the first of a fine collection!

MY TIPS

~~~

1

To select the right book, make sure it contains more words than pictures.

2

After your first question, refine the message received by repeating the experiment several times (but don't overdo it) by asking for clarification or by asking a further question.

PRESIDENTIAL BIBLIOMANCY

Abraham Lincoln, the 16th president of the United States of America, is said to have practised bibliomancy. To obtain an accurate interpretation of his dreams, he would open the Bible and let his fingers run down the page until they reached the divine message.

YOUR BRILLIANT MENTAL FLEXIBILITY: ASC AND THE TRANCE STATE

I am sure you will have realised by now that received wisdom has a hard time of it with me! Imagine a hard toffee. If you find a good way of warming it up, it can soften very quickly. Then you can do anything you like with it, or nearly anything. It is the same with our minds! They have an incredible capacity for flexibility. We can come up with several options to solve the same problem, adopt multiple different ways of doing things, but also think outside the box and outside the norm. This flexibility is essential when it comes to interpreting synchronicities.

MENTAL MAGNETISM

Mental magnetism, also known as cerebral or suggestive magnetism, is a magnetism that is exclusively used under the influence of the human being. When our mind is focused and concentrated on a particular thought, as when it is under hypnosis, a mental magnetism is triggered. It is up to the individual whether they use this to a positive or negative end. This form of magnetism has no limit in terms of time or distance. It is practised by everyone, whether consciously or otherwise.

🐚 A naturally magical state

There is no need to be a great meditator or practised hypnotherapist to experience the hypnotic trance state. Did you know that every day, we experience this state approximately every 90 minutes? Have you ever noticed that your gaze has been 'blocked' for a moment, that you were immersed in a film until you forgot the world around you, or that your car drove you to your destination by itself? If the answer is yes to any of these, then, you were in a light trance. When we are absorbed in something, absent-minded or in a daydream, we are probably experiencing this naturally magical state without being aware of it.

Despite common belief, when we experience the altered state of consciousness (ASC) of trance, it does not mean that we are asleep and can no longer react to something important. As an example of this, let me tell you about two experiences during consultations a few years ago. During a reiki session with a client, when a delivery man knocked loudly on my door, we heard absolutely nothing. But on another occasion, with another client, a burning smell immediately brought us out of a deep trance.

This is why I would advise you not to listen to people who project their fears by telling you that therapies such as hypnosis can make you do almost anything. When we are in a hypnotic trance, we are in an awakened state of consciousness, that is to say that our unconscious mind is no longer fettered by our conscious mind.

It is important to note that our unconscious mind is responsible for 95% of our lives. This covers our learning, our memory, the perceptions of our five senses, our ability to adapt and update our beliefs on the basis of our frame of reference. By dissociating the conscious from the unconscious, we have even more control over ourselves, our desires, our needs and our objectives. In a trance state, you will never do anything that runs contrary to your personal values and limits.

🗨 Signs of a light trance

- Blood circulation increases, so the complexion becomes pink or red.
- Muscles relax, which can cause your eyes to water.
- Swallowing becomes more regular.
- Slight involuntary spasms may occur.
- Heart and breathing rates are variable.
- Pupils are dilated and the gaze unfocused.
- Rapid eye movements give the impression that the person is about to fall asleep.
- The five senses undergo changes.
- The little voice inside changes (becomes louder or is totally absent).

People who are particularly Cartesian or controlling are less easily hypnotised, as they are less 'influenceable'. This is why they will let go more easily and be more receptive to ASC when they are tired.

MY TIPS

1

Practise self-hypnosis throughout the day. Ideally, take advantage of the troughs in the ultradian cycles (part of the 90-minute biorhythm that repeats itself day and night) during which our state of consciousness naturally changes – an example of this would be when you have difficulty concentrating and read the same paragraph four times without anything going in!

2

If you do the Live Deeply in the Moment exercise on the opposite page at the right time of day for 15 minutes, it helps you to recover more easily from sleep deprivation.

3

At the end of the experience, if you are having trouble 'coming back', visualise a means of transport, a ladder or a bridge to help you.

LIVE DEEPLY IN THE MOMENT

Here is a practical exercise that will allow you to experience a light trance. The aim is to help you take full advantage of the present moment and increase your alertness to interpreting synchronicities.

Before you begin, decide on your objective. It might be to make a decision, to relax, to listen to your feelings or to clarify a problematic situation. The formulation of your wish must be active and positive. Avoid any 'don'ts'.

1. Settle yourself very comfortably indoors or in location that brings you closer to nature. Adopt the position that will relax you the most quickly, without going to sleep. You may be laying down or seated.

2. Close your eyes, centre yourself and take three deep, long breaths.

3. Before you enter the trance state, remind yourself of your objective and lay it at the door of your unconscious mind. Anchor it in a place that you love (your garden, a golden sandy beach, etc.) and be creative (colour in the letters, make it 3D, use contrasting sizes, etc.).

4. With your conscious mind, repeat your objective to yourself at least three times, like a mantra.

5. Then imagine a staircase leading you towards your inner garden. Let your mind guide you in the direction of the welcoming environment of your choice.

6. Allow your senses to absorb its atmosphere. What can you see? What can you hear? Is there a distinctive fragrance? Observe, without reflecting, and let yourself go.

7. Are you alone? Is there a person or animal nearby? If there is, ask them if they have a message or answer to give you. If there are no living beings, take this time for yourself, connect with the sensations you are experiencing.

8. When you feel it is time, come back up the staircase to return to the here and now. Open your eyes in your own time and note down in your little notebook what you have just experienced.

THE POWER OF EXPRESSING GRATITUDE

Saying thank you: this sign of courtesy is often thought of as a mere polite gesture, an acknowledgement or sometimes even a dismissal; however, it has a much deeper power. By being grateful to something or someone (including yourself), whatever the intention behind the thanks, the simple fact of voicing it shows the receiver that we have taken it into account, and this is important. This 'thank you' validates the existence of what they have said or done. When expressed consciously and from the heart, this appreciation is invaluable in human relationships (in the family, at the office, etc.). Nothing and no one is perfect, including life itself. Even if life is not always rosy, comfortable and sweet, be grateful for it, because that in itself will make you happy! Yes, you did read that correctly! Numerous scientific studies on the subject show that when we express our gratitude or appreciation, we contribute directly to our individual and collective well-being.

100% GRATITUDE

French novelist Marcel Proust said, 'Let us be grateful to the people who make us happy; they are the charming gardeners who make our souls blossom.' And it appears to be scientifically proven. According to the *Clinical Psychology Review*, 'in recent years, many studies have clearly demonstrated the links between gratitude and many forms of well-being.' So, let us turn to our notebooks. Every day, write a spontaneous list of five situations, people or events for which you feel grateful. As the weeks go by, you will discover new things about yourself, about your passions and even those interests which you had never previously considered.

Go ahead and express your gratitude, wherever you are and whatever the situation you are in. Even in the most serious of endeavours and most formal of meetings, gratitude for a sunny day or for seeing a beautiful painting in a waiting room will always have a positive impact. Believe me, I've experienced it!

Bathe in gratitude by swapping 'To be happy, I want...' for 'I am happy to have or to be...'. This does not prevent you from having dreams, targets and objectives. Quite the contrary, it will ensure you have the motivation you need for your projects. You will not be stimulated by fear or the fact that you are missing something, but by a new opportunity to experience joy and make other people happy. Far from being illusory magical thinking that erases our sorrows

DAMAGED EGO

Many people think they do not have to thank others because they are under the impression that they are giving more than they are receiving. When we think this way, it means that our ego is being deeply impacted. An old wound or trauma is being revived. While not excusing this behaviour, the narcissistic and individualistic society in which we live and the merit system that goes with it does not help.

and concerns, expressing gratitude helps us to maintain a constantly more positive and confident state of mind. As a result, you will find yourself in a virtuous circle that will naturally increase your capacity to grasp great opportunities linked to synchronicities.

23:00
THE NIGHT: ATTRACTING SYNCHRONICITY TO YOU

What a crazy day! The time has come to take stock. Having appreciated, observed, explored and interpreted synchronicity, you may think that it holds no further secrets for you. However, in the following pages, the night will reveal a new facet of this phenomenon that may well surprise you.

RENDERING THE UNCONSCIOUS CONSCIOUS

We discussed the notion of the unconscious on page 100 when we talked about our brilliant mental flexibility with the ASC and the hypnotic trance state. For Carl Gustav Jung, 'Until you make the unconscious conscious, it will direct your life and you will call it fate.' In order to make our unconscious conscious and thus grasp the reins of our life (biological, chemical, behavioural and mental functions), it is essential to recognise the power of our unconscious.

In terms of memory, our unconscious is easily a match for powerful computers and brilliant innovations in artificial intelligence.

By contrast, its modelling strategies and means of operating are not always as efficient as we would like them to be. Let me explain. I like to represent the unconscious as a five-year-old child. At this age children are changing daily: they are a sponge for everything they see around them and they are progressively fashioning their own judgement and reasoning. They are loyal and faithful, following the principles of education, society and the environment that they experience. By feeding their frame of reference (a kind of personal hard drive), they adopt behaviours and reactions accordingly, as their over-arching desire is to ensure survival. They reject anything they may identify as a danger, using all means at their disposal, even a psychsomatic illness (that tummy ache before a spelling test, for example).

It is important to note, that the unconscious mind does not like to complicate life. It favours routine and seeks simplicity, pleasure and ease in all circumstances. And if it does not have any new models or new inspiration to model itself on, it does not change.

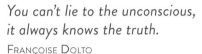

You can't lie to the unconscious,
it always knows the truth.

FRANÇOISE DOLTO

The way in which the unconscious mind reasons sometimes makes no sense to our conscious (logical and rational) mind. For example, just over five years ago I decided to try hypnotherapy to kick my smoking habit. After the second session, I had given up for good. Together with the hypnotherapist, we had discovered that my unconscious had found an unhelpful coping mechanism in response to my sister being very ill at the time. This action was smoking two to three packets a day. You might say this is illogical, but for my unconscious mind, this reason was a very valid one. It had done its best on the basis of its experience and its frame of reference at the time. I am sharing this personal anecdote with you to illustrate my point. Letting go of obsolete programs and loading new ones in our unconscious is therefore possible at any time.

WAKING DREAMS

Another very significant method for rendering the unconscious conscious was developed by the French psychotherapist Georges Romey (1929-2019), and that is the free waking dream, inspired by the method developed by Robert Desoille in the 1920s. I highly recommend Romey's book *Rêve Éveillé Libre, une nouvelle voie thérapeutique* [translates to: *Free Waking Dreaming: a new therapeutic approach*].

THE FILM OF YOUR DAY

Before you go to sleep at night, settle down comfortably and close your eyes. Calmly take several long, deep breaths. Relax and go back in time. Moment by moment, scene by scene, replay the film of your day, from getting up until the present moment. Then open your eyes. In your little notebook, write down (a sentence, a word) or draw (an object, a symbol, a colour) something that best represents the hours you consciously experienced. In the same way, jot something down that describes the hours that passed where you did not manage to savour their rightful value. Visualise very specifically what you have written down or drawn for the hours lived consciously, then let your most faithful ally, your unconscious mind, do the rest.

In addition, I would advise you to visualise and become aware of the moments when you were on 'autopilot' (for example on public transport or during a work meeting). What might you have felt if you had been more present in that moment? What would your mental, emotional or physical sensations have been? Go to sleep anchoring down the intention of being more conscious the next day when you wake up.

THE POWER OF INTENTION

For the Indian-American doctor and writer Deepak Chopra, everything that happens in the Universe begins with an intention: 'When I decide to buy a birthday present, wiggle my toes, or call a friend, it all starts with intention.' When we are connected to the power of intention, a benevolent harmony reigns in us and around us. It empowers us, inspires us, brings us joy, and ensures that our life's events are positively aligned. Once again, there's no magic recipe or miraculous gift. We all have the ability to connect to this inexhaustible source, although you may find the WWWWHHW (or 'questioning method') helpful to pin things down.

WWWWHHW

WHO?
For whom? Is it for you alone?

WHAT?
Describe the subject of your intention.

WHERE?
In which place specifically?

WHEN?
Starting from when? Until what date?

HOW? HOW MUCH/MANY?
The methods and the means. The number is important, particularly if your intention is related to the energy of money.

WHY?
Your reasons, your causes, your objectives.

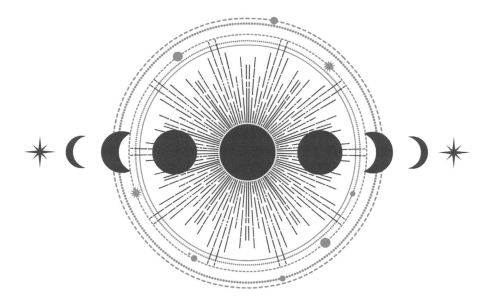

When I work with my coachees, I start to explore the power of intention with them by suggesting the following exercise. I ask them to describe to me what they would like to obtain. Responses vary, of course: more money, more self-confidence or even a lovely car. We make a note of it. Then, depending on their answer, I immediately give the coachee what they wished for. I take a dollar coin out of my pocket, or offer them a small toy car, for example. Their reaction wavers between surprise and incomprehension. Then, I generally ask them if they would like something to drink. Without asking them more specifically about what they would like, I offer them a glass of iced water in winter and a steaming cup of tea in summer. Once again, they don't understand. Then I tell them that I have given them what they wanted: a drink.

So, in order to get what we really want and aspire to, it is essential to set out your clear, precise and detailed intention. Wanting more money then becomes a monthly increase of €200. More self-confidence turns into personalised image consultation, and the lovely car into a search for a blue, 4-door, 5-seater car costing a maximum of €15,000. The more you are able to visualise your intention, the more chance you have of achieving it. To see is to know, to want is to be able and to dare is to really have.

LAW OF ATTRACTION: BECOMING A MAGNET FOR SYNCHRONICITIES

When interviewed about his art in 1936, Pablo Picasso said, 'I do not seek. I find.' The artist was unknowingly applying one of the tenets of the Law of Attraction: be positive!

We can all create our own reality in order to attract synchronicities to us. 'Ask and you shall receive' and 'You reap what you sow', are sayings which we can believe in and make come true. Our daily lives can change dramatically if we practise them regularly.

What you think, you become.
What you feel, you attract.
What you imagine, you create.
FRANCK NICOLAS

☁ My 4 tenets of the law of attraction

1. Create the ideal conditions. Opt for a zen attitude, let go and have patience. The effects of the law of attraction will not arrive when you decide they will. Go with the rhythm of the Universe and surf on the flow of life so as not to get bogged down.

2. Venture outside your comfort zone and dare! If you always do the same thing, you will get the same result. So think and act differently.

3. Be positive. Use positive words and structure your phrases in the same way. For example, you no longer want to eat sweets, but you do want to free yourself from the grip of sugar. Remember that your brain does not understand the 'do nots'.

4. Believe in yourself, in this method and in life! Despite the obstacles in your path, do not lose sight of your goal. It is okay to feel tired, angry or sad. But after expressing your emotions, put them into perspective by seeing this problem as an opportunity to develop new resources.

The law of attraction will never be synonymous with perfection

Doing everything you can to attract life's gifts to you is all well and good, but what if the surprise you receive is not the one you were expecting? Accept that every experience is for a reason. Sometimes we don't understand why until years later, when we will be grateful for having experienced that sudden change, accident or break-up.

Celebrated Spanish singer-songwriter Julio Iglesias would certainly back me on this. While studying to become a diplomat, he proved himself to be a talented footballer. He was destined for a professional career with Real Madrid. But a serious car accident put an end to his sporting career and left him immobilised for two years. The nurse in charge of his care gave him a guitar. He started to play and then to sing. When he finished his law studies in 1968, he entered a major singing competition in Spain, and that was the start of his stellar career! If he had not suffered his accident, would Julio Iglesias have become a musician?

BENEFICIAL CRISIS

The word for crisis in Chinese 危机 is a synonym for opportunity. The Hebrew word for crisis, *mashber*, connotes a notion of rebirth, renewal and innovation.

DEVELOPING YOUR POSITIVE THOUGHTS THROUGH PREMONITORY DREAMS

Before you fall into the arms of Morpheus, let me share a last practical exercise with you. It is done in three phases.

☁ Phase 1:
the positive request

Sleep allows our body to rest and our energies to regenerate. Our brain, however, never stops, even when we are in the deepest of sleeps. So the night is the perfect time to make your positive requests. Be sure to have them in your head just before you turn out the light, but only after you have closed your book or turned off your television. Choose a meditative time when all is peaceful.

☁ Phase 2:
the dream journal

Keep a notepad and pen in your bedside cabinet. You will use it as a diary to record any dreams that you remember. Even if they seem confused, lacking in detail and illogical, write down anything you have seen, heard or felt during your dream, without judgement. If you are more auditory than visual, use the dictaphone function on your smartphone to describe your dream experience. Keeping a record will allow you to commit your dreams to memory more easily.

☁ Phase 3:
reinforcing by speaking out loud

In order to deeply anchor and enhance your dreams, recount them to a trusted friend or family member. Describe in the greatest detail what you have experienced. The only rule to respect is not to seek to decode, interpret or analyse your dream. Ask this person to listen attentively without interruption as you allow the energy of the dream to act on you. They can then put any questions they have to you and ask for clarification before describing the feeling that these images provoke. The aim here is to help you take a step back from what you have just experienced so you can see things from a different angle.

IN SUMMARY

To be anchored is to be rooted in, attached to and consciously connected with the Earth and the present moment.

As reality is not the 'true' reality, it is essential that you rely on your own personal experience and frame of reference to properly experience synchronicities, remembering that our perception is totally subjective. Synchronicity is a muscle that you need to work for it to develop. This can be done in particular by (re)connecting to and developing your five senses.

Messages from the Universe can take different forms. They may be written (word, letter, number, etc.), visual (symbol, colour, material, etc.), oral (speech, radio or television programme) or artistic expressions (song, dance, painting, etc.), but no one medium is stronger than another. When the same message comes to you more than twice in a short period of time it is of great importance.

Every 90 minutes, we experience an altered state of consciousness (ASC), which is a light trance. The law of attraction will never be synonymous with perfection. Remain open to the idea of receiving a surprise which at first glance is not to your liking. Every experience is for a reason.

As your vibrations increase, you will be carried along with the current and things will come to you effortlessly.

SANDY FORSTER

FURTHER INFORMATION

CONCLUSION

Make the magic yours. Become the magician of your life.

This is what I have wished for throughout the month and a half that I dedicated to writing this book.

I have a deep belief in the power of words, especially when they are written. They are genuine portals to the wider world and to our own, inner world.

I am passionate about teaching and it has been a great pleasure to write this book. I hope it has fulfilled your needs and answered your questions. If at least one of you has been able to enjoy what all these discoveries have allowed me to become, I will feel I have done my job.

We are all unique and different. In the course of our lives, we evolve, we are enriched and we transform. The truth for us today may be different tomorrow or indeed remain the same. There is no wrong decision or wrong move, simply life experience. I believe that no method or technique can be the best or the most successful and suit everyone. Spreading this knowledge is in my opinion like passing on the flaming torch. So now it is up to you to decide, in your own way, your relationship with synchronicities. Reading this book is just a very small step along your life's journey. From now on, the rest is up to you. It is up to you to practise and train. My only advice is to seek constantly to push the boundaries of your knowledge. Learning is continually understanding and questioning yourself so you never find yourself resting on your laurels.

I wish you lots of enriching experiences and discoveries. Never forget that you are the co-creator of your life. You have control of your destiny, so it is up to you!

Life is like a magician. It draws your attention to one thing in order to distract you from another.
Francis Machabée

When you open yourself up to synchronicity, it is for life, for its power is infinite. I've just had such an intense synchronic experience that I cannot resist sharing it with you. Yesterday, I spent a very large part of my afternoon carefully rereading the manuscript of this book, reviewed and corrected by the talented Annabelle. At about 7pm, I decided to do something else so I got on with the personalised numerological study that I am currently working on.

When I work in numerology, I find myself in a light trance state. We can all experience this hypnotic state when we are particularly concentrated and focused. Sometimes I even forget the name of the person I am studying, as was the case last night. When I supplement the results of personalised numerological studies with information from my intuitive channel, I often receive messages and have 'flashes' about my clients or myself.

Yesterday, at about 9pm, as I was busy writing, I felt I had to stop immediately. My mind was asking me to reconnect with a childhood memory. I found myself in front of the gates of a school in the small town where I grew up in the suburbs of Paris. I then saw the face of a girl who had been at the school at the time, more than 20 years ago. Her first and last name appeared before my eyes: Éloïse D.

To try and understand why I had had this 'flash', I decided to search for her on the internet. A few clicks later, I found that someone by this name with a profile similar to hers was friends with Lucie, one of my French friends living in Quebec! Note I had lived in Montreal for almost three years.

Lucie, who is always helpful, responsive and open-minded, listened to my story. She confirmed that she knew Éloïse very well and that she, like us, was of French origin. Indeed, Éloïse, like me, had immigrated to the Quebec region in September 2018. Extraordinary but true!

My soul overflowed with joy! What if it was the same Éloïse D.? The synchronicity would be extraordinary! I searched my memory for any more information on Éloïse D. that I could give Lucie. I could clearly visualise her father's physique and personality, but could not think of his name. I went off to have my shower and at 22.22 hrs precisely, as I stood under the jet of water, I had another flash 'Eric! Eric D.!' I threw on my dressing gown and found on LinkedIn that it was indeed him.

And as we say in Quebec, here's the 'cherry on top of the sundae', as I was sorting through the pages of the numerology study I was working on, I found that one of the first names of the consultants was... Éloïse! This morning, Lucie confirmed that it was indeed the same Éloïse D. with whom I had been a girl scout... 23 years ago! How amazing is that?

ACKNOWLEDGEMENTS

The Universe, for its multiple synchronicities that have appeared in my path to spur me on since 2012, and particularly during the writing of this book.

My invisible, but illuminating and benevolent companions, for allowing me to share my knowledge humbly with a wider audience, in Europe and Quebec, and especially my grandmother.

All the people who contributed to this book, on both sides of the Atlantic, in particular my editor Vanessa for her faith in me.

Annabelle, for her invaluable proofreading and loyalty since the very beginning.

Alexandra, for her magnificent and utterly inspiring illustrations.

All the honest, kind and professional people I have met in the fields of personal development, natural health and well-being for almost ten years, but also the jealous, envious and manipulative people who have crossed my path.

My husband, for following me with so much love for so many years.

My actual family, the people who feel like my family, and my close friends for their support, especially Mathilde and Bouchra.

Sylvie, my first coach, through whom I discovered the power of synchronicity.

All my clients, coachees and colleagues.

Anyone who did not believe in me in the past, who does not today, and who may even not in the future. Thanks also to those who, by contrast, have trusted me blindly.

And finally, a huge THANKS to someone you know well: you! Without readers, there are no authors!

Like many of the best things in life, the most precious are not always what you were looking for but those that arrive by themselves when you were looking for something else.
BENJAMIN N. CARDOZO

BIBLIOGRAPHY

Find Your Purpose, Change Your Life: Getting to the Heart of Your Life's Mission
Carol Adrienne
Published by William Morrow Paperbacks (an imprint of HarperColllins), 2011

Meaningful Coincidences: How and Why Synchronicity and Serendipity Happen
Bernard Beitman, M.D.
Published by Park Street Press, 2022

The Serendipity Mindset: The Art and Science of Creating Good Luck
Dr. Christian Busch
Published by Penguin Life, 2020

Synchronicity: The Marriage of Matter and Psyche
F. David Peat
Published by Pari Publishing, 2015

Signs: The Secret Language of the Universe
Laura Lynne Jackson
Published by Piatkus, 2019

Secrets of Spirit Communication: Techniques for Tuning In and Making Contact
Trish MacGregor and Rob MacGregor
Published by Llewellyn Publications, 2018

The Four Agreements: A Practical Guide to Personal Freedom
Don Miguel Ruiz
Published by Amber-Allen Publishing, 2018

Sidewalk Oracles: Playing with Signs, Symbols, and Synchronicity in Everyday Life
Robert Moss
Published by New World Library, 2015

The Power of Letting Go
John Purkiss
Published by Aster, 2020

The Conscious Universe: The Scientific Truth of Psychic Phenomena
Dean Radin
Published by HarperOne, 2010

Supernormal: Science, Yoga, and the Evidence for Extraordinary Psychic Abilities
Dean Radin
Published by Deepak Chopra, 2013

The Child In You: The Breakthrough Method for Bringing Out Your Authentic Self
Stefanie Stahl
Published by Penguin Life, 2021

Necessary Chances: Synchronicity in the Encounters That Transform Us
Jeff Vézina
Published by Pari Publishing, 2022

MY EXPERIENCES WITH SYNCHRONICITY

Taking inspiration from page 15, list and date below all the examples of synchronicities in your daily life. Then compare them, identifying common points and repetitions.

_____

_____

_____

_____

_____

_____

_____

_____

_____

_____

_____

_____

_____

_____

5 SENSES IN 5 EXERCISES

Referring to pages 57 and 58, fill in each of your sensory experiences.

1. TASTE

2. SMELL

3. SIGHT

4. HEARING

5. TOUCH

MIRROR HOURS

List the mirror, double or twin hours that you encounter below. Refer to pages 71 to 82 to discover their meaning.

TO INCREASE SYNCHRONICITIES IN MY LIFE

* Bibliomancy (page 98)
* ASC and the trance state (page 100)
* Gratitude (page 105)

Participate in *bookcrossing*
(also known as BC or BX or book swap)
by sending a book on a journey. This
worldwide phenomenon seeks to
circulate books by 'releasing' them into
the world, on a park bench, for example,
or on the underground, in a taxi, on a
café terrace, so that they can be read
by other people who will go on to
're-release' them in turn...

INDEX

active listening 58
altered states of consciousness (ASCs)
    100–1, 106, 113, 117
anchoring 44–5, 47
animal symbolism 88–91
Attraction, Law of 110–11

beliefs 38–41, 53–4
bibliomancy 94, 98–9

Campbell, Joseph 24, 25
causality 22
chance 16–18
change 34–7, 85
clouds, symbolism of 85
coincidence 16–18
collective unconscious 21, 23, 25, 49
connectedness 46, 49
'critical mass' thesis 46

divination 92–9
dreams, premonitory 112

ego 105
emotions 31, 36–7
energy, indestructible 22
equilibrium, personal 30, 34–6

failure 35–6
feathers 49, 85–7
fine structure constant 82

'going with the flow' 35
gratitude practice 104–5
grounding 44–5, 47
guides 13–14

healing 75
hundredth monkey, story of 46
hypnotic trance 100–2, 106–7, 117

I Ching 23, 93–6
inner child 37, 68
inspiration 76
intention 108–9
intuition 63, 67

Jung, Carl Gustav 9, 13, 20–3, 25, 37,
    69, 71, 88, 92–4

Kammerer, Paul 20–1
Koestler, Arthur 83, 98

luck 16–18

magic 16–18, 37, 116
meditation, tree-rooting 45
mental magnetism 100
messages 69–70, 113
miracles 16–18
mirror hours 71–82
mood books 36
morphic resonance 48

needs, personal 30, 34–6
negativity 36, 39, 54, 66
neuro-linguistic programming (NLP) 50
notebooks 36–7, 56, 67, 70, 103, 105, 108, 112
numerology 71–82, 117

openness 34
oracles 97

paranormal 32, 37
past lives 74
Pauli, Wolfgang Ernst 20, 22, 25, 82
positivity 8, 34, 36, 39, 110, 112
praying mantis 24
prediction 69
premonition 112

radiesthesia 63
repetition 83

scarab beetles 23
scientific evidence 38
senses 56–61, 67
Seriality, Law of 20–1
Sheldrake, Rupert 48

sixth sense 63, 67
slips of the tongue 70–1
social synchronicity 46
space-time-continuum 22
state of mind 29, 34
superstition 69–70

totem animals 90
trance 100–3, 106–7, 113, 117
trickster, the 71

unconscious 21, 23, 25, 34, 36, 49, 70, 100–1, 103, 106–8
Universe 18, 20–1, 23, 49, 68–70, 113

vibratory rate 63–6

world maps, personal 50

A DAVID AND CHARLES BOOK
© 2022, Secret d'étoiles, Paris
www.secretdetoiles.com

David and Charles is an imprint of David and
Charles, Ltd, Suite A, Tourism House, Pynes Hill,
Exeter, EX2 5WS

Originally published in France in 2022 as Décryptez
les messages de l'Univers
First published in the UK and USA in 2023

Anne-Sophie Casper has asserted her right to be
identified as author of this work in accordance with
the Copyright, Designs and Patents Act, 1988.

A catalogue record for this book is available from
the British Library.

ISBN-13: 9781446309872 paperback

This book has been printed on paper from
approved suppliers and made from pulp from
sustainable sources.

MIX
Paper from
responsible sources
FSC
www.fsc.org
FSC® C012521

Printed in China through Asia Pacific Offset for:
David and Charles, Ltd, Suite A, Tourism House,
Pynes Hill, Exeter, EX2 5WS

10 9 8 7 6 5 4 3 2 1

Photos : Shutterstock
Illustrations © Alexandra Alzieu : 22, 35, 51,
64-65, 95

Director : Guillaume Pô
Editorial Director : Élisabeth Pegeon
Editorial Design : Vanessa Martel assisted by
Marianne Louis
Copy Preparation : Annabelle Biau-Weber
Artistic Direction : Julie Mathieu
Cover Design : Caroline Soulères
Layout Design : Stéphanie Boulay
Production Manager : Thierry Dubus
Production : Florence Bellot

David and Charles publishes high-quality books on
a wide range of subjects. For more information visit
www.davidandcharles.com

Follow us on Instagram by searching for
@dandcbooks_wellbeing

Layout of the digital edition of this book may vary
depending on reader hardware and display settings.